POWER

FROM

God

POWER
FROM
God

CHARLES FINNEY

Whitaker House

Unless otherwise indicated, all Scripture quotations are taken from the *King James Version* (KJV) of the Bible.

Scripture quotations marked (RV) are taken from the *Revised Version* of the Holy Bible.

POWER FROM GOD
(previously titled *Power from on High*)

ISBN: 0-88368-631-7
Printed in the United States of America
Copyright © 1996 by Whitaker House

Whitaker House
30 Hunt Valley Circle
New Kensington, PA 15068

Library of Congress Cataloging-in-Publication Data

Finney, Charles Grandison, 1792–1875.
  Power from God / by Charles Finney.
    p. cm.
  ISBN 0-88368-631-7 (alk. paper)
  1. Christian life—Congregational authors. 2. Holy Spirit. I. Title.
  BV4501.2 .F4846   2000
  248.4'858—dc21   00-011030

1 2 3 4 5 6 7 8 9 10 11 / 09 08 07 06 05 04 03 02 01 00

CONTENTS

– 1 –
POWER FROM ON HIGH

POWER FROM ON HIGH

Please permit me to correct a misunderstanding by some of the members of the late council at Oberlin. This misunderstanding arose from the brief remarks that I made to them, first on a Saturday morning and afterward on Sunday. In my first remarks to them, I called attention to the mission of the church to disciple all nations, as recorded by Matthew and Luke. I stated that this commission was given by Christ to the whole church, and that every member of the church is obligated to make it his lifework to convert the world. I then raised two questions: (1) What do we need to ensure success in this great work? (2) How can we get it?

The Promise of the Father

The answer to the first question is this: we need to be clothed with *"power from on high"* (Luke 24:49). During His ministry, Christ had informed the disciples that without Him they could do nothing (John 15:5). Just before His ascension, when He gave them the commission to convert the world, He added, *"Behold, I send the promise of my Father upon you: but tarry ye in the city of Jerusalem, until ye be endued with power from on high"* (Luke 24:49). He also said, *"Ye shall be baptized with the Holy Ghost not many days hence"* (Acts 1:5). This baptism of the Holy Spirit, this thing promised by the Father, this outpouring of power from on high, is essential. Christ has expressly informed us that it is the indispensable condition of doing the work He gave us.

Consecration, Prayer, Supplication

How will we get power from on high? Christ expressly promised it to the whole church and to everyone who has the duty to labor for the conversion of the world. He admonished the first disciples not to undertake the work until they had received this outpouring of power from on high. Both the promise and the admonition apply equally to all Christians of every age and nation. No one has, at any time, any right to expect success unless he first obtains this outpouring of power from on high. The example of the first disciples teaches us how to obtain this outpouring. They first consecrated themselves to this work. Then they continued in prayer and supplication (see Acts 1:14) until the Holy Spirit fell upon them on the Day of Pentecost, and they received the promised outpouring of power from on high. This, then, is the way to get it.

> The promise and the admonition apply to all Christians of every age and nation.

The council desired me to say more upon this subject. Consequently, on Sunday, I took for my text the statement of Christ that the Father is more willing to give the Holy Spirit to those who ask Him than we are to give good gifts to our children. (See Luke 11:13.)

I said that this text informs us that it is infinitely easy to obtain the Holy Spirit, or this outpouring of power from the Father. I also said that this outpouring is made a constant subject of prayer for many people. Everybody prays for this repeatedly, and yet, with all this intercession, how comparatively few are really clothed with this spiritual power from on high! This need is not being met. Lack of power is a subject of constant complaint. Christ says, *"Every one that asketh receiveth"* (Matthew 7:8), but there certainly is a great gulf between the asking and receiving that is a sizable stumbling block to many.

Why the Outpouring of the Spirit Is Not Received

How, then, is this discrepancy to be explained? I then proceeded to show why this outpouring is not received. I gave many reasons.

First, we are not willing, on the whole, to have what we desire and ask for. Second, God has expressly informed us that if we regard iniquity in our hearts, He will not hear us (Psalm 66:18). But the petitioner is often self-indulgent. This is iniquity, and God will not hear him.

I gave many more reasons. The petitioner is uncharitable. He is critical. He is self-dependent.

He resists conviction of sin. He refuses to confess to all parties concerned. He refuses to make restitution to injured parties.

11

He is prejudiced and biased. He is resentful. He has a revengeful spirit. He has a worldly ambition. He has committed himself on some point and has become dishonest because he neglects and rejects further light. He is denominationally selfish. He is selfish for his own congregation.

He resists the teachings of the Holy Spirit. He grieves the Holy Spirit by dissension. He quenches the Spirit by persistence in justifying wrong. He grieves Him by a lack of watchfulness. He resists Him by yielding to an evil temper.

He is dishonest in business. He is lazy and impatient in waiting on the Lord. He has selfishness that takes on many forms. He is negligent in business, in study, in prayer. Or he undertakes too much business, too much study, and too little prayer. He lacks entire consecration.

Last and greatest, He has *unbelief*. He prays for this outpouring without expecting to receive it. *"He that believeth not God hath made him a liar"* (1 John 5:10). This, then, is the greatest sin of all. What an insult, what a blasphemy, to accuse God of lying!

I was obliged to conclude that these and other forms of indulged sin explain why so little is received, while so much is asked. I said I had not time to present the other side. Some of the believers afterward inquired, "What is the other side?" The other side presents the certainty that we will receive the promised outpouring of power from on high, and be successful in winning souls, if we ask, and if we fulfill the plainly revealed conditions of prevailing prayer. Observe that what I said on Sunday was on the same subject and in addition to what I had previously said. The council's misunderstanding was this: If we first get rid of all these forms of sin, which prevent our receiving this outpouring, have we not already obtained the blessing? What more do we need?

The Difference between Peace and Power

The answer is this: there is a great difference between the *peace* and the *power* of the Holy Spirit in the soul. The disciples were Christians before the Day of Pentecost, and, as such, had a measure of the Holy Spirit. They must have had the peace of sins forgiven and of a justified state, but yet they did not have the infusion of power necessary to do the work assigned them. They had the peace that Christ had given them but not the power that He had promised.

> Seek until you obtain the outpouring of power from on high.

This may be true of all Christians, and this is, I think, the great mistake of the church and of the ministry. People rest in conversion, and they do not continue by seeking until they obtain this outpouring of power from on high. Hence, so many professors of Christianity have no power with either God or man. They prevail with neither. They cling to a hope in Christ, and even enter the ministry, overlooking the admonition to wait until they are clothed with power from on high. But if someone brings all the tithes and offerings into God's treasury, if he lays all upon the altar and puts God to the test by doing so, he will find that God will "*open* [to him] *the windows of heaven, and pour* [him] *out a blessing, that there shall not be room enough to receive it*" (Malachi 3:10).

– 2 –
SAVING IMPRESSIONS

– 2 –

SAVING IMPRESSIONS

The apostles and believers received it on the Day of Pentecost. What did they receive? What power did they exercise after that event? They received a powerful baptism of the Holy Spirit, a vast increase of divine illumination.

This baptism imparted a great diversity of gifts that were used for the accomplishment of their work. It clearly included many outward things. The power of a holy life. The power of a self-sacrificing life. (The manifestation of these must have greatly influenced those to whom they proclaimed the Gospel.) The power of a cross-bearing life. The power of great meekness, which this baptism enabled them everywhere to exhibit. The power of a loving enthusiasm in proclaiming the Gospel. The power of teaching. The power of a loving and living faith. The gift of tongues. An increase of power to work miracles. The gift of inspiration, or the revelation of many truths before unrecognized by them. The power of moral courage to proclaim the Gospel and do the bidding of Christ, whatever it cost them.

What Christ Has Promised

In their circumstances, all these gifts were essential to their success, but neither separately nor all together did they constitute the power from on high that they manifestly received. What they manifestly received as the supreme, crowning, and all-important means of success was the power to prevail with both God and man, the power to fasten saving impressions on the minds of men. This was doubtless the thing that they understood Christ to promise. He had commissioned the church to convert the world to Himself. Everything that I named above were only means, which could never secure the end unless they were vitalized and made effective by the power of God. The apostles, no doubt, understood this, and, laying themselves and their all upon the altar, they entreated the throne of grace in the spirit of entire consecration to their work.

> The disciples received the power to prevail with both God and man.

They did, in fact, receive the gifts before mentioned; but, supremely and principally, they received this power to make saving impressions on men. It was manifested right on the spot. They began to address the multitude, and, wonderful to tell, three thousand were converted the same hour. But, observe, no new power was manifested by them upon this occasion, except the gift of tongues. They worked no miracle at that time, and they used these tongues simply as the means of making themselves understood.

Please note that they had not had time to exhibit any other gifts of the Spirit that I have named above. They did not at that time have the advantage of exhibiting a holy life or any of the powerful graces and gifts of the Spirit. What was said on the occasion, as recorded in the book of Acts, was said with a new power; otherwise, it could not have made a saving impression on the people.

This power was not the power of inspiration, for they only declared certain facts of their own knowledge. It was not the power of human learning and culture, for they had but little. It was not the power of human eloquence, for there appears to have been but little of it. It was God speaking in and through them. It was a power from on high—God in them making a saving impression on those to whom they spoke.

Power That Cuts to the Heart

This power to make a saving impression stayed with and upon them. It was, no doubt, the great and main thing promised by Christ and received by the apostles and early Christians. It has existed, to a greater or lesser extent, in the church ever since. It is a mysterious fact often manifested in a most surprising manner. Sometimes, a single sentence, a word, a gesture, or even a look will convey this power in an overcoming manner.

To the honor of God alone, I will say a little about my own experience in this matter. I was powerfully converted on the morning of the tenth of October. In the evening of the same day and on the morning of the following day, I received overwhelming baptisms of the Holy Spirit, which went through me, as it seemed to me, body and soul. I immediately found myself clothed with such power from on high that a few words dropped here and there to individuals were the means of their immediate conversion. My words seemed to fasten like barbed arrows in the souls of men. They cut like a sword. They broke the heart like a hammer. Multitudes can attest to this. Oftentimes, a word dropped, without my remembering it, would fasten conviction and often result in almost immediate conversion.

Sometimes, I would find myself, in a great measure, empty of this power. I would go out and visit and find that I made no saving impression. I would exhort and pray with the same result. I would then set apart a day for private fasting and prayer, fearing that this power had departed from me, and would inquire anxiously after the reason of this apparent emptiness. After humbling myself and crying out for help, the power would return upon me with all its freshness. This has been my experience throughout my life.

I could fill a volume with the history of my own experience and observation with respect to this power from on high. It is a fact of consciousness and of observation, but it is a great mystery. I have said that sometimes a look has in it the power of God. I have often witnessed this. Let the following fact illustrate it.

I once preached, for the first time, in a mill town. The next morning, I went into the manufacturing establishment to view its operations. As I passed into the weaving department, I saw a large group of young women, some of whom, I observed, were looking at me, and then at each other, in a manner that indicated a frivolous spirit and that also showed they knew me. I, however, knew none of them. As I approached nearer to those who had recognized me, they seemed to become more silly and giddy. Their levity made a peculiar impression on me; I felt it in my heart. I stopped short and looked at them, with what expression I do not know because my whole mind was absorbed with the sense of their guilt and danger.

As I steadily looked at them, I observed that one of them became very much agitated. A thread broke. She attempted to mend it, but her hands trembled in such a manner that she could not do it. I immediately observed that the sensation was spreading and had become universal among the group. I looked steadily at them until one after another gave up and paid no more attention to their looms. They fell on their knees, and the influence spread throughout the whole room. I had not spoken a word, and the noise of the looms would have prevented my being heard if I had.

> They fell on their knees, and the influence spread throughout the whole room.

In a few minutes, all work was abandoned, and tears and lamentations filled the room. At this moment, the owner of the factory, who was himself an unsaved man, came in, accompanied, I believe, by the superintendent, who was a professed Christian. When the owner saw the state of things, he said to the superintendent, "Stop the mill." What he saw seemed to pierce him to the heart.

"It is more important," he hurriedly remarked, "that these souls should be saved than that this mill should run." As soon as the noise of the machinery had ceased, the owner inquired, "What should we do? We must have a place to meet where we can receive instruction."

The superintendent replied, "The mule room will do." The mules were placed out of the way, and all of the employees were notified and assembled in that room. We had a marvelous meeting. I prayed with them and gave them such instruction as at the time they could bear. The Word was with power. Many expressed hope in Christ that day; and within a few days, as I was informed, nearly every person in that great establishment, together with the owner, had hope in Christ.

The Marvels of the Spirit's Power

This power is a great marvel. I have many times seen people unable to endure the Word. The most simple and ordinary statement would cut men off from their seats like a sword, take away their bodily strength, and render them almost as helpless as dead men. Several times, it has been true in my experience that I could not raise my voice, or say anything in prayer or exhortation except in the mildest manner, without wholly overcoming those who were present. This was not because I was preaching terror to the people; rather, the sweetest sounds of the Gospel would overcome them.

This power seems sometimes to pervade the atmosphere of one who is highly charged with it. Many times, great numbers of people in a community are clothed with this power, and the very atmosphere of the whole place seems to be charged with the life of God. Strangers coming into it and passing through the place are instantly struck with conviction of sin and, in many instances, converted to Christ.

When Christians humble themselves and consecrate their all afresh to Christ and ask for this power, they will often receive such a baptism that they will be instrumental in converting more souls in one day than in all their lifetimes before. While Christians remain humble enough to retain this power, the work of conversion will go on until whole communities and regions of the country are converted to Christ. The same is true of ministers and laity alike.

– 3 –

THE SPIRIT FALLS ON SODOM

The Spirit Falls on Sodom

S ince the publication in the *Independent* of my article "The Power from on High," I have been confined with a prolonged illness. In the meantime, I have received numerous letters of inquiry on the subject. Some of these letters ask for further illustrations of the exhibition of this power. In response to this question, I will relate another exhibition of this power from on high, as witnessed by myself.

Soon after I was licensed to preach, I went into a region of the country where I was a total stranger. I went there at the request of a female missionary society located in Oneida County, New York. Early in May, I think, I visited the town of Antwerp in the northern part of Jefferson County. I stopped at the village hotel and there learned that there were no religious meetings being held in that town at that time. They had a brick meetinghouse, but it was locked up. By personal efforts, I got a few people to assemble in the living room of a Christian lady in the place, and I preached to them on the evening after my arrival.

As I walked around the village, I was shocked at the horrible profanity that I heard among the men wherever I went. I obtained permission to preach in the schoolhouse on the next Sunday; but before that Sunday arrived, I was very discouraged and almost terrified, in view of the state of society that I witnessed. On Saturday, the Lord applied with power to my heart the following words, addressed by the Lord Jesus to Paul: *"Be not afraid, but speak, and hold not thy peace: for I am with thee, and no man shall set on thee to hurt thee: for I have much people in this city"* (Acts 18:9–10). This completely subdued my fears, but my heart was loaded with agony for the people.

On Sunday morning, I rose early and retired to a grove not far from the village to pour out my heart before God for a blessing on the labors of the day. I could not express the agony of my soul in words, but struggled with much groaning and, I believe, with many tears, for an hour or two, without getting relief. I returned to my room in the hotel, but almost immediately came back to the grove. This I did three times. The last time, I got complete relief, just as it was time to go to the meeting.

I went to the schoolhouse and found it filled to its capacity. I took out my little pocket Bible and read for my text, *"God so loved the world, that he gave his only begotten Son, that whosoever believeth in him should not perish, but have everlasting life"* (John 3:16). I set forth the love of God as contrasted with the way He was treated by those for whom He gave up His Son. I charged them directly with their profanity; and, as I recognized among my hearers several whose profanity I had particularly noticed, in the fullness of my heart and the flowing of my tears, I pointed to them and said, "I heard these men call upon God to condemn their fellow man." The Word took powerful effect. Nobody seemed offended, but almost everybody greatly melted.

At the close of the service, the amiable landlord, Mr. Copeland, rose and said he would open the meetinghouse in the afternoon. He did so. The meetinghouse was full, and, as in the morning, the Word took powerful effect. Thus, a powerful revival commenced in the village, which soon after spread in every direction.

I think it was on the second Sunday after this, when I finished preaching in the afternoon, that an aged man approached and said to me, "Can you come and preach in our neighborhood? We have never had any religious meetings there." I asked the direction and the distance and made an appointment to preach there the next afternoon, Monday, at five o'clock, in their schoolhouse. I had preached three times in the village and attended two prayer meetings on Sunday, and on Monday I went on foot to fulfill this appointment.

Since the weather was very warm that day, I felt almost too weary to walk, and I was greatly discouraged before I arrived. I sat down in the shade by the wayside and felt as if I were too faint to continue. I felt that, if I did, I was too discouraged to talk to the people. When I finally arrived, I found the house to be filled, and I immediately started the service with a hymn. The people attempted to sing, but the horrible discord agonized me beyond expression. I leaned forward, put my elbows on my knees and my hands over my ears, and shook my head to shut out the discord, which I could barely endure. As soon as they had stopped singing, I got on my knees, almost in a state of desperation. The Lord opened the windows of heaven upon me and gave me great liberty and power in prayer.

Up to that moment, I had no idea what text I should use on the occasion. As I rose from my knees, the Lord gave me this: *"Up, get you out of this place; for the LORD will destroy this city"* (Genesis 19:14). I told the people, as nearly as I could recollect, where they would find this passage, and I went on to tell them of the destruction of Sodom. I gave them an outline of the history of Abraham and Lot and their relations to each other, of Abraham's praying for Sodom, and of Lot being the only pious man who was found in the city.

"I was struck with the fact that the people looked exceedingly angry at me."

While I was doing this, I was struck with the fact that the people looked exceedingly angry at me. Many faces looked very threatening, and some of the men looked as if they were about to strike me. This I could not understand, because I was only giving them, with great liberty of spirit, some interesting sketches of Bible history. As soon as I had completed the historical sketch, I turned to them and said that I had understood they had never had any religious meetings in that neighborhood. I then applied that fact as I thrust at them with the sword of the Spirit with all my might.

From that moment, the solemnity increased with great rapidity. In a few moments, an instantaneous shock seemed to fall upon the congregation. I cannot describe the sensation that I felt, nor that which was apparent in the congregation, but the Word seemed literally to cut like a sword. The power from on high came down upon them in such a torrent that they fell from their seats in every direction. In less than a minute, nearly all the people in the congregation were either down on their knees or on their faces or in some position prostrate before God. Everyone was crying or groaning for mercy upon his own soul. They paid no further attention to me or to my preaching. I tried to get their attention, but I could not.

I observed the aged man who had invited me there as still retaining his seat near the center of the house. He was staring around him with unutterable astonishment. Pointing to him, I cried at the top of my voice, "Can't you pray?" He knelt down and roared out a short prayer about as loud as he could holler, but they paid no attention to him.

After looking around for a few moments, I knelt down and put my hand on the head of a young man who was kneeling at my feet and engaged in prayer for mercy on his soul. I got his attention and preached Jesus in his ear. In a few moments, he seized Jesus by faith and then broke out in prayer for those around him. I then turned to another in the same way, with the same result, and then another, and another, until I do not know how many had laid hold of Christ and were full of prayer for others. After continuing in this way until nearly sunset, I was forced to commit the meeting to the charge of the old gentleman who had invited me because I had to go to fulfill an appointment in another place in the evening.

In the afternoon of the next day, I was requested to hurry back to this place because they had not been able to break up the meeting. They had been asked to leave the schoolhouse to give place to the school, but they had moved to a private house nearby. There I found a number of people still too anxious and too much loaded down with conviction to go to their homes. These were soon subdued by the Word of God, and I believe all obtained a hope before they went home.

Observe that I was a total stranger in that place. I had never seen nor heard of it before that time. However, during my second visit, I learned that the place was called Sodom by reason of its wickedness, and the old man who invited me was called Lot because he was the only believer in that place.

After that meeting, revival broke out in the old man's entire neighborhood.

I have not been in that neighborhood for many years; but in 1856, I think, while I was laboring in Syracuse, New York, I was introduced to a minister by the name of Cross, from St. Lawrence County. He said to me, "Mr. Finney, you don't know me, but do you remember preaching in a place called Sodom?"

I said, "I will never forget it."

He replied, "I was then a young man and was converted at that meeting." He is still living, is a pastor in one of the churches in that county, and is the father of a principal in our school. Those who have lived in that region can testify to the permanent results of that blessed revival. I can only give in words a feeble description of that wonderful manifestation of power from on high that attended the preaching of the Word.

– 4 –

Conditions of Receiving Power

– 4 –

Conditions of Receiving Power

In this chapter, I propose to consider the conditions on which this outpouring of power can be obtained. Let us borrow a little light from the Scriptures. I will not encumber you with quotations from the Bible, but simply state a few facts that will readily be recognized by all readers of the Scriptures. If you will read in the last chapters of Matthew and of Luke the commission that Christ gave to His disciples, and, in connection, will read the first and second chapters of the book of Acts, you will be prepared to appreciate what I have to say at this time.

First of all, the disciples had already been converted to Christ, and their faith had been confirmed by His resurrection. But here let me say that conversion to Christ is not to be confused with a consecration to the great work of the world's conversion. In conversion, the soul deals directly and personally with Christ. It yields up its prejudices and its selfishness, accepts Him, trusts Him, and supremely loves Him. All this the disciples had, more or less, distinctly done; but they had not received a definite commission yet or a particular infusion of power to fulfill a commission.

However, when Christ had dispelled their great bewilderment resulting from His crucifixion, and confirmed their faith by repeated interviews with them, He gave them the Great Commission to win all nations to Himself. But He admonished them to wait at Jerusalem until they were clothed with power from on high, which He said they should receive in a few days.

Now, observe what they did. They assembled, the men and women, for prayer. They accepted the commission. No doubt, they came to an understanding of the nature of the commission and the necessity of the spiritual outpouring that Christ had promised. As they continued day after day in prayer and self-examination, they, no doubt, came to appreciate more and more the difficulties that would beset them and to feel more and more their inadequacy to the task.

One must conclude that they, one and all, consecrated themselves, with all they had, to the conversion of the world as their lifework. They must have renounced utterly the idea of living for themselves in any form. They must have devoted themselves with all their powers to the work set before them. Logically speaking, this consecration, this self-renunciation, this dying to the world, must have preceded their actual seeking of the promised power. They then continued, with one accord, in prayer for the promised baptism of the Spirit, which included all that was essential to their success.

> The disciples consecrated themselves, with all they had, to the conversion of the world as their lifework.

Observe that they had a work set before them, and they had a promise of power to perform it. They were admonished to wait until the promise was fulfilled. How did they wait? Not in listlessness and inactivity. Not in making preparations by study and otherwise to get along without it. Not by going about their business and offering an occasional prayer that the promise might be fulfilled. Rather, they continued in prayer and persisted in their petitions until the answer came. They understood that it was to be a baptism of the Holy Spirit. They understood that it was to be received from Christ. They prayed in faith. They held on with the firmest expectation until the outpouring came. Now, let these facts instruct us as to the conditions of receiving this outpouring of power.

We Have the Same Commission

First, we, as Christians, have the same commission to fulfill. As truly as they did, we need an outpouring of power from on high. Of course, the same admonition, to wait on God until we receive it, is given to us.

We Have the Same Promise

Second, we have the same promise that they had. Now, let us take substantially and in spirit the same course that they did. They were Christians and had a measure of the Spirit to lead them in prayer and in consecration. So have we. Every Christian possesses a measure of the Spirit of

Christ, enough of the Holy Spirit to lead us to true consecration and inspire us with the faith essential to prevail in prayer. Let us, then, not grieve or resist Him, but accept the commission and fully consecrate ourselves, with all we have, to the saving of souls as our great and our only lifework. Let us go to the altar with all that we have and are, and let us lie there and persist in prayer until we receive the outpouring.

Again, conversion to Christ is not to be confused with the acceptance of this commission to convert the world. The first is a personal transaction between the soul and Christ, relating to its own salvation. The second is the soul's acceptance of the service in which Christ proposes to employ it.

Christ does not require us to make brick without straw. To whom He gives the commission He also gives the admonition and the promise. If the commission is heartily accepted, if the promise is believed, if the admonition to wait upon the Lord until our strength is renewed is complied with, we will receive the outpouring.

We Are Given This Commission Individually

Third, it is of supreme importance that all Christians should understand that this commission to convert the world is given to them by Christ individually.

Everyone has the great responsibility passed on to him or her to win as many souls as possible to Christ. This is the great privilege and the great duty of all the disciples of Christ. There are a great many departments in this work. But in every department, we may and ought to possess this power so that, whether we preach, pray, write, print, trade, travel, take care of children, administer the government of the state, or whatever we do, our whole lives and influence should be permeated with this

> Whatever we do, our whole lives and influence should be permeated with the power of God.

power. Christ says, *"He that believeth on me,...out of his belly shall flow rivers of living water"* (John 7:38). That is, a Christian influence, having in it the element of power to impress the truth of Christ upon the hearts of men, will proceed from him.

The Great Needs of the Church Today

The church has great needs at present. First, it needs the clear conviction that this commission to convert the world is given to each of Christ's disciples as his lifework. I fear I must say that the great mass of professing Christians seem never to have been impressed with this truth. They leave the work of saving souls to ministers.

The second great need is a clear conviction of the necessity of this outpouring of power upon every individual soul. Many professing Christians suppose it belongs especially and only to preachers. They fail to realize that all believers are called to preach the Gospel, that the whole life of every Christian is to be a proclamation of the glad tidings.

A third need is an earnest faith in the promise of this outpouring. A great many professing

Christians, and even ministers, seem to doubt whether this promise is to the whole church and to every Christian. Consequently, they have no faith to grasp it. If it does not belong to all, they do not know to whom it does belong. So, naturally, they cannot grasp the promise by faith.

A fourth need is persistence in waiting on God for the power, as is commanded in the Scriptures. Many faint before they have prevailed, and hence the outpouring is not received. Multitudes seem to be satisfied with hoping for eternal life for themselves. They never get ready to move beyond the question of their own salvation and to leave that as settled with Christ. They do not get ready to accept the Great Commission to work for the salvation of others because their faith is so weak that they are unsure of their own salvation. They do not steadily leave the question of their own salvation in the hands of Christ. Even some ministers of the Gospel, I find, are in the same condition and are halting in the same way. These ministers are unable to give themselves wholly to the work of saving others because they are somewhat unsure of their own salvation.

It is amazing to witness how much the church has practically lost sight of the necessity of this outpouring of power. Almost everybody speaks much of our dependence on the Holy Spirit, but how little this dependence exists. Christians and even ministers go to work without it. I mourn that I must say that the ranks of the ministry seem to be filling up with those who do not possess it. May the Lord have mercy on us! Will this last remark be thought unloving? If so, let the report of the Home Missionary Society, for example, be heard on this subject. Surely, something is wrong.

An average of five souls won to Christ by each missionary of that Society in a year's toil certainly indicates a most alarming weakness in the ministry. Have all or even a majority of these ministers been clothed with the power that Christ promised? If not, why not? But if they have, is this all that Christ intended by His promise?

I have previously said that the reception of this infusion of power is instantaneous. I do not mean that in every instance the recipient was aware of the precise time at which the power began to work mightily within him. It may have begun like the dew and increased to a shower.

I have alluded to the report of the Home Missionary Society. Not that I suppose that the brothers in Christ employed by that society are exceptionally weak in faith and power as laborers for God. On the contrary, from my acquaintance with some of them, I regard them as among our most devoted and self-denying laborers in the cause of God. This fact illustrates the alarming weakness that pervades every branch of the church, both clergy and laity. Are we not weak? Are we not criminally weak?

> We need an earnest faith in the promise of the outpouring of the Spirit.

It has been suggested that, by writing this way, I would offend the ministry and the church. I cannot believe that the statement of so palpable a fact will be regarded as an offense. The fact is, there is something sadly defective in the education of the ministry and of the church. The ministry is weak because the church is weak. And then, again, the church is kept weak by the weakness of the ministry. Oh, for a conviction of the necessity of this outpouring of power and a faith in the promise of Christ!

–5–
Is It a Hard Saying?

Is It a Hard Saying?

I have previously said that the lack of an infusion of power from on high is a disqualification for a pastor, a deacon or elder, a Sunday school superintendent, a professor in a Christian college, and especially for a professor in a theological seminary. Is this a hard saying? Is this an unloving saying? Is it unjust? Is it unreasonable? Is it unscriptural?

Suppose any one of the apostles, or those present on the Day of Pentecost, had failed through apathy, selfishness, unbelief, indolence, or ignorance to obtain this outpouring of power. Would it have been uncharitable, unjust, unreasonable, or unscriptural to have counted him disqualified for the work to which Christ had appointed him?

Christ had plainly told His disciples that without this infusion of power, they could do nothing. He had plainly commanded them not to attempt the work in their own strength, but to wait at Jerusalem until they received the necessary power from on high. He had also plainly promised that, if they waited, in the sense that He intended, they should receive it *"not many days hence"* (Acts

1:5). They evidently understood Him to command them to wait in the sense of a constant waiting upon Him in prayer and supplication for the blessing. Now, suppose that any one of them had stayed away and attended to his own business, waiting for the sovereignty of God to confer this power. He, of course, would have been disqualified for the work; and if his fellow Christians, who had obtained this power, had deemed him so, would it have been uncharitable, unreasonable, unscriptural?

Is not the same true for all who are commanded to disciple the world, those who were promised this power? If, through any shortcoming or fault of theirs, they fail to obtain this gift, are they not disqualified for the work and especially for any official position? Are they not, in fact, disqualified for leadership in the sacramental host? Are they not disqualified as teachers of those who are to do the work? If it is a fact that they lack this power, however this defect is to be accounted for, it is also a fact that they are not qualified to be teachers of God's people. And if they are seen to be disqualified because they lack this power, it must be reasonable and right and scriptural so to deem them, and so to speak of them, and so to treat them.

Who has a right to complain? Surely they do not. Should the church of God be burdened with teachers and leaders who lack this fundamental qualification, when their failing to possess it must be their own fault? It is truly amazing to see the obvious apathy, indolence, ignorance, and unbelief that exist on this subject. They are inexcusable.

They must be highly criminal. With such a command to convert the world ringing in our ears; with such an admonition to wait in constant, wrestling prayer until we receive the power; with such a promise, made by such a Savior, held out to us, a promise of all the help we need from Christ Himself, what excuse can we offer for being powerless in this great work? What an awe-inspiring responsibility rests upon us, upon the whole church, upon every Christian!

One might ask, How is apathy, how is indolence, how is the common, fatal neglect possible under such circumstances? If any of the early Christians to whom this commandment was given had failed to receive this power, would we not think them greatly to blame? If such default had been sin in them, how much more in us, with all the light of history and of fact blazing upon us that they had not received? Some ministers and many Christians treat this matter as if it were to be left to the sovereignty of God without any persistent effort to obtain this power. Did the early Christians so understand and treat it? No, indeed. They gave themselves no rest until this baptism of power came upon them.

> The early Christians did not rest until they received the baptism.

I once heard a minister preaching on the subject of the baptism of the Holy Spirit. He treated it as a reality, and when he came to the question of how it was to be obtained, he said truly that it was to be obtained as the apostles obtained it on the Day of Pentecost. I was very gratified, and I listened eagerly to hear him press the obligation on his hearers to give themselves no rest until they had obtained it. But in this I was disappointed; for before he sat down, he seemed to relieve the audience from the feeling of obligation to obtain the baptism and left the impression that the matter was to be left to the discretion of God. He said what seemed to imply a censure of those who vehemently and persistently urged God to fulfill the promise. Nor did he hold out to them the certainty of their obtaining the blessing if they fulfilled the conditions. The sermon was in most respects a good one, but I think the audience left without any feeling of encouragement or sense of obligation to seek the baptism earnestly.

This is a common fault of the sermons that I hear. They are very instructive, but they fail to leave the congregation with either a sense of obligation or a feeling of great encouragement to use the necessary means. They are greatly defective in their concluding remarks. They neither leave the conscience under a pressure nor the whole mind under the stimulus of hope. The doctrine is often good, but the "what then?" is often left out.

Many ministers and professors of religion seem to be theorizing, criticizing, and endeavoring to justify their neglect of this attainment. The apostles and other Christians did not do so. The attainment was not a question that they tried to grasp with their intellects before they embraced it with their hearts. It was with them, as it should be with us, a question of faith in a promise. I find many people trying to grasp with their intellect, and settle as theory, questions of pure experience. They are puzzling themselves by trying to comprehend with the mind what is to be received as a conscious experience through faith.

There is need of a great reformation in the church on this particular point. Churches should wake up to the facts in the case and take a new position, a firm stand in regard to the qualifications of ministers and church officers. They should refuse to settle on a man as pastor if they are unsure he has power to win souls. Whatever else he may have to recommend him, if his record does not show that he has this infusion of power to win souls to Christ, they should deem him unqualified. Churches used to have a customary practice, and I believe some still do, in presenting a call to the pastorate. Having witnessed the spiritual fruits of the candidate's labors, they would certify that they deemed him qualified and called of God to the work of the ministry. Churches should be well satisfied in some way that they are calling a *fruitful* minister and not a dry stalk—that is, a mere intellect, a mere head with little heart; an elegant writer, but with no fervency; a great logician, but of little faith; a fervid imagination, perhaps, but with no Holy Spirit power.

Churches should hold the theological seminaries to a strict account in this matter; and until they do, I fear the theological seminaries will never wake up to their responsibilities. Some years ago, one branch of the Scottish church was very disturbed with the lack of fervency and power in the ministers supplied to them by their theological seminary. They passed a resolution that until the seminary reformed in this respect, they would not employ ministers who were educated there. This was a necessary, a just, a timely rebuke, which I believe was very beneficial. A theological seminary ought by all means to be a school not merely for the teaching of doctrine, but also, and even more especially, for the development of Christian experience. Of course, students should receive a good education in those schools, but it is immeasurably more important that they should be led to a thorough personal knowledge of Christ and those things found in Philippians 3:10:

> *That I may know* [Christ], *and the power of his resurrection, and the fellowship of his sufferings, being made conformable unto his death.*

A theological seminary that aims mainly at the culture of the intellect and sends out learned men who lack this infusion of power from on high is a snare and a stumbling block to the church. The seminaries should recommend no one to the churches, however great his intellectual attainments, unless he has this most essential of all attainments, the infusion of power from on high. Seminaries should be judged as incompetent to educate men for the ministry if it is seen that they send out men as ministers without this power. Churches should inform them-selves and look to those seminaries that furnish not merely the best educated but also the most earnest and spiritually powerful ministers.

> Culture and intellect alone are not needed— we need an infusion of power from on high.

It is amazing that, while it is generally admitted that the outpouring of power from on high is a reality, and essential to ministerial success, that it should be practically treated by churches and by schools as of comparatively little importance. In theory, it is admitted to be everything; but, in practice, it is treated as if it were nothing. From the days of the apostles to the present day, it has been seen that men of very little human culture, but clothed with this power, have been highly successful in winning souls to Christ, while men of the greatest learning, with all that the schools have done for them, have been powerless so far as the proper work of the ministry is concerned. And yet we go on laying ten times more stress on human culture than we do on the baptism of the Holy Spirit. Practically, human culture is treated as infinitely more important than the infusion of power from on high.

Most seminaries are furnished with learned men, but often not with men of spiritual power; hence, they do not insist upon this infusion of power as indispensable to the work of the ministry. Students are pressed almost beyond endurance with study and developing the intellect, while scarcely an hour in a day is given to instruction in Christian experience. Indeed, I do not know if even one course of lectures on Christian experience is given in the theological seminaries. But religion is an experience. It is a consciousness. Personal fellowship with God is the secret of the whole of it. There is a world of most essential learning in this direction that is wholly neglected by the theological seminaries. With them, doctrine, philosophy, theology, church history, and sermonizing are everything, and real heart-union with God is nothing.

Spiritual power to prevail with God and to prevail with man has but little place in their teaching.

I have often been surprised at the judgments men form in regard to the prospective usefulness of young men preparing for the ministry. Even professors are very apt, I see, to deceive themselves on this subject. If a young man is a good scholar, a fine writer, and makes good progress in biblical interpretation, they have strong hopes for him. These professors must know that, in many such cases, these young men cannot pray—that they have no fervency, no power in prayer, no spirit of wrestling, of agonizing and prevailing with God. Yet they are expecting them, because of their intellects, to make their marks in the ministry and to be highly useful.

For my part, I expect no such thing of this class of men. I have infinitely more hope for the usefulness of a man who, at any cost, will keep up daily fellowship with God; who is yearning for and struggling after the highest possible spiritual attainment; who will not live without daily persistence in prayer and being clothed with power from on high.

Churches, presbyteries, associations, and whoever licenses young men for the ministry are often very faulty in this respect. They will spend hours in informing themselves of the intellectual culture of the candidates, but scarcely as many minutes in ascertaining their heart culture—what they know of the power of Christ to save from sin, what they know of the power of prayer, and whether and to what extent they are clothed with power from on high to win souls to Christ. The whole proceedings on such occasions leave the impression that human learning is preferred to spiritual fervency. Oh, that it were different, and that we were all agreed, practically, now and forever, to hold fast to the promise of Christ and never think ourselves or anybody else to be fit for the great work of the church until we have received a rich outpouring of power from on high.

I beg my brothers in Christ, and especially my younger brothers in Christ, not to think these things were written in the spirit of reproach. I beg the churches, I beg the seminaries, to receive a word of exhortation from an old man who has had some experience in these things and whose heart mourns and is weighed down because of the shortcomings of the church, the ministers, and the seminaries on this subject. Fellow believers, I implore you to consider this matter more thoroughly, to wake up and take it to heart. Do not rest until this subject of the outpouring of power from on high is brought forward into its proper place. Do not rest until it takes that prominent and practical position in the view of the whole church that Christ intended it should.

– 6 –
PREVAILING PRAYER

– 6 –

PREVAILING PRAYER

Prevailing prayer is that which gets an answer. Saying prayers is not offering prevailing prayer. The effectiveness of prayer does not depend so much on quantity as on quality. I do not know how better to approach this subject than by relating a fact of my own experience before I was converted. I relate it because I fear such experiences are too common among the unsaved.

I do not remember ever having attended a prayer meeting until after I began the study of law. Then, for the first time, I lived in a neighborhood where there was a weekly prayer meeting. I had neither known, heard, nor seen much of religion; hence, I had no definite opinions about it. Partly from curiosity and partly from an uneasiness of mind on the subject, which I could not well define, I began to attend that prayer meeting. About the same time, I bought the first Bible that I ever owned, and I began to read it. I listened to the prayers that I heard offered in those prayer meetings with all the attention that I could give to prayers so cold and formal. In every prayer, they prayed for the gift and outpouring of the Holy Spirit. Both in their prayers and in their remarks, which were occasionally interspersed, they acknowledged that they did not prevail with God. This was most evident and had almost made me a skeptic.

Seeing me so frequently in their prayer meeting, the leader, on one occasion, asked me if I wanted them to pray for me. "No," I replied. "I suppose that I need to be prayed for, but your prayers are not answered. You confess it yourselves." I then expressed my astonishment at this fact, in view of what the Bible said about the effectiveness of prayer.

Indeed, for some time, my mind was much perplexed and in doubt in view of Christ's teaching on the subject of prayer and the obvious facts before me from week to week in this prayer meeting. Was Christ a divine Teacher? Did He actually teach what the Gospels attributed to Him? Did He mean what He said? Did prayer really avail to obtain blessings from God? If so, what was I to make of what I witnessed from week to week and month to month in that prayer meeting? Were they real Christians? Was what I heard real prayer in the Bible sense? Was it such prayer as Christ had promised to answer? Here I found the solution.

I became convinced that they were under a delusion, that they did not prevail because they had no right to prevail. They did not comply with the conditions on which God had promised to hear prayer. Their prayers were just the kind God had promised *not* to answer. It was evident they were overlooking the fact that they were in danger of praying themselves into skepticism in regard to the value of prayer.

Conditions of Having Our Prayers Answered

In reading my Bible, I noticed many revealed conditions of having our prayers answered. I will explain these conditions in this chapter.

Expecting to Receive What We Ask For

Faith in God as the One who answers prayer is one condition. This, it is plain, involves the expectation of receiving what we ask for.

Asking according to God's Will

Another declared condition is asking according to the revealed will of God. This plainly implies not only asking for such things as God is willing to grant, but also asking in such a state of mind as God can accept. I fear that it is common for professed Christians to overlook the state of mind in which God requires them to be as a condition of answering their prayers.

Sincerity

It is plain that sincerity is a condition of prevailing with God. Take, for example, the phrase *"Thy kingdom come"* (Matthew 6:10) from the Lord's Prayer. Sincerity in offering this petition implies the whole heart and life devotion of the petitioner to the building up of this kingdom. It implies the sincere and thorough consecration of all that we have and all that we are to this end. To utter this petition in any other state of mind involves hypocrisy and is an abomination.

The same is true with the next petition, *"Thy will be done in earth, as it is in heaven"* (Matthew 6:10). God has not promised to hear this petition unless it is sincerely offered. But sincerity implies a state of mind that accepts the whole revealed will of God, so far as we understand it, as it is accepted in heaven. It implies a loving, confiding, universal obedience to the whole known will of God, whether that will is revealed in His Word, by His Spirit, or in His providence. It implies that we hold ourselves, and all that we have and are, as absolutely and cordially at God's disposal as do the inhabitants of heaven. If we fall short of this and withhold anything whatsoever from God, we *"regard iniquity in* [our] *heart*[s]*"* (Psalm 66:18), and God will not hear us.

> Sincerity implies a state of mind that accepts the whole revealed will of God.

Sincerity in offering this petition implies a state of entire and universal consecration to God. Anything short of this is withholding from God what is His due. It is turning away our ears from hearing the law. But what do the Scriptures say? *"He that turneth away his ear from hearing the law, even his prayer shall be abomination"* (Proverbs 28:9). Do professed Christians understand this?

What is true of offering these two petitions is true of *all* prayer. Do Christians take this to heart? Do they consider that all professed prayer is an abomination if it is not offered in a state of entire consecration of all that we have and are to God? If we do not offer ourselves and all that we have as we pray, if we are not in a state of mind that cordially accepts and, so far as we know, perfectly conforms to the whole will of God, our prayer is an abomination. How greatly profane is the use very frequently made of the Lord's Prayer, both in public and in private. To hear men and women chatter through the Lord's Prayer, *"Thy kingdom come. Thy will be done in earth, as it is in heaven"* (Matthew 6:10), while their lives are anything but conformed to the known will of God, is shocking and revolting. To hear men pray *"Thy kingdom come"* while it is most evident that they are making little or no sacrifice or effort to promote this kingdom, forces the conviction of barefaced hypocrisy. Such is not prevailing prayer.

Unselfishness

Unselfishness is a condition of prevailing prayer. *"Ye ask, and receive not, because ye ask amiss, that ye may consume it upon your lusts"* (James 4:3).

A Clear Conscience

Another condition of prevailing prayer is a conscience void of offense toward God and man.

> For if our heart [conscience] condemn us,
> God is greater than our heart, and knoweth

> *all things. Beloved, if our heart condemn us not, then have we confidence toward God. And whatsoever we ask, we receive of him, because we keep his commandments, and do those things that are pleasing in his sight.* (1 John 3:20–22)

Here two things are made plain: first, that to prevail with God, we must keep a conscience void of offense; second, we must keep His commandments and do those things that are pleasing in His sight.

A Pure Heart

A pure heart is also a condition of prevailing prayer. *"If I regard iniquity in my heart, the Lord will not hear me"* (Psalm 66:18).

Confession and Restitution

All due confession and restitution to God and man is another condition of prevailing prayer. *"He that covereth his sins shall not prosper: but whoso confesseth and forsaketh them shall have mercy"* (Proverbs 28:13).

Clean Hands

Clean hands is another condition. *"I will wash mine hands in innocency: so will I compass thine altar, O LORD"* (Psalm 26:6). *"I will therefore that men pray every where, lifting up holy hands, without wrath and doubting"* (1 Timothy 2:8).

Reconciliation among Believers

The settling of disputes and animosities among believers is a condition.

Therefore if thou bring thy gift to the altar, and there rememberest that thy brother hath ought against thee; leave there thy gift before the altar, and go thy way; first be reconciled to thy brother, and then come and offer thy gift. (Matthew 5:23–24)

Humility

Humility is another condition of prevailing prayer. *"God resisteth the proud, but giveth grace unto the humble"* (James 4:6).

Removing Stumbling Blocks

Taking away the stumbling blocks is another condition.

Son of man, these men have set up their idols in their heart, and put the stumbling-block of their iniquity before their face: should I be inquired of at all by them? (Ezekiel 14:3)

Forgiveness

A forgiving spirit is a condition. *"Forgive us our debts, as we forgive our debtors"* (Matthew 6:12). *"But if ye forgive not men their trespasses, neither will your Father forgive your trespasses"* (Matthew 6:15).

A Truthful Spirit

The exercise of a truthful spirit is a condition. *"Behold, thou desirest truth in the inward parts"* (Psalm 51:6). If the heart is not in a truthful state, if it is not entirely sincere and unselfish, we regard iniquity in our hearts; therefore, the Lord will not hear us.

Praying in Christ's Name

Praying in the name of Christ is a condition of prevailing prayer.

The Inspiration of the Holy Spirit

The inspiration of the Holy Spirit is another condition. All truly prevailing prayer is inspired by the Holy Spirit.

> *For we know not what we should pray for as we ought: but the Spirit itself maketh intercession for us with groanings which cannot be uttered. And he that searcheth the hearts knoweth what is the mind of the Spirit, because he maketh intercession for the saints according to the will of God.*
> (Romans 8:26–27)

This is the true spirit of prayer. This is being led by the Spirit in prayer. It is the only really prevailing prayer. Do professed Christians really understand this? Do they believe that unless they live and walk in the Spirit, unless they are taught how to pray by the intercession of the Spirit in them, they cannot prevail with God?

Fervency

Fervency is a condition. A prayer, to be prevailing, must be fervent.

Confess your faults one to another, and pray one for another, that ye may be healed. The effectual fervent prayer of a righteous man availeth much. (James 5:16)

Perseverance

Perseverance or persistence in prayer is often a condition of prevailing. See the case of Jacob, of Daniel, of Elijah, of the Syrophenician woman, the parable of the unjust judge, and the teaching of the Bible in general.

Travail of Soul

Travail of soul is often a condition of prevailing prayer. *"As soon as Zion travailed, she brought forth her children"* (Isaiah 66:8). Paul said, *"My little children, of whom I travail in birth again until Christ be formed in you"* (Galatians 4:19). This implies that he had travailed in birth for them before they were converted. Indeed, travail of soul in prayer is the only real revival prayer. If anyone does not know what this is, he does not understand the spirit of prayer. He is not in a revival state. He does not understand the passage already quoted—Romans 8:26–27. Until he understands this agonizing prayer, he does not know the real secret of revival power.

The Consistent Use of Means

Another condition of prevailing prayer is the consistent use of means (resources, such as money, energy, time) to obtain the object prayed for. Means should be used if they are within our reach and are known by us to be necessary to obtain the end. To pray for a revival of religion and use no other means is to tempt God.

This, I could plainly see, was the case of those who offered prayer in the prayer meeting of which I have spoken. They continued to offer prayer for a revival of religion, but outside of the meeting they were as silent as death on the subject and did not open their mouths to those around them. They continued in this inconsistency until a prominent sinner in the community administered a terrible rebuke to them in my presence. He expressed just what I deeply felt. He rose and, with the utmost solemnity and tearfulness, said, "Christian people, what can you mean? You continue to pray in these meetings for a revival of religion. You often exhort each other here to wake up and use means to promote a revival. You assure each other, and assure us who are unrepentant, that we are on the way to hell; and I believe it. You also insist that if you should wake up and use the appropriate means, there would be a revival and we would be converted. You tell us of our great danger and that our souls are worth more than all worlds, and yet you keep busy in your comparatively trifling activities and use no such means. We have no revival, and our souls are not saved."

Here he broke down and fell, sobbing, back into his seat. This rebuke fell heavily upon that prayer meeting, as I will ever remember. It did them good; for it was not long before the members of that prayer meeting broke down, and we had a revival. I was present in the first meeting in which the revival spirit was evident. Oh, how changed was the tone of their prayers, confessions, and supplications. In returning home, I remarked to a friend, "What a change has come over these Christians. This must be the beginning of a revival."

> A wonderful change comes over prayer meetings whenever Christians are revived.

Yes, a wonderful change comes over all the meetings whenever Christian people are revived. Then their confessions mean something. They mean reformation and restitution. They mean work. They mean the use of means. They mean the opening of their pockets, their hearts, and their hands, and the devotion of all their powers to the promotion of the work.

Specificity

Another condition of prevailing prayer is that it is specific. It is offered for a definite object. We cannot prevail for everything at once. In all the cases recorded in the Bible in which prayer was answered, it is noteworthy that the petitioner prayed for a definite object.

Speaking from the Heart

Another condition of prevailing prayer is that we mean what we say in prayer, that we make no false pretenses—in short, that we are entirely childlike and sincere, speaking out of the heart, saying nothing more or less than we mean, feel, and believe.

Believing That God Keeps His Word

Another condition of prevailing prayer is a state of mind that assumes the good faith of God in all His promises.

Watching and Praying in the Holy Spirit

Another condition is *"watch*[ing] *unto prayer"* (1 Peter 4:7) as well as *"praying in the Holy Ghost"* (Jude 20). By this, I mean guarding against everything that can quench or grieve the Spirit of God in our hearts. Also, I mean watching for the answer in a state of mind that will diligently use all necessary means, at any expense, and add entreaty to entreaty.

When the fallow ground is thoroughly broken up in the hearts of Christians, when they have confessed and made restitution—if the work is thorough and honest—they will naturally and inevitably fulfill the conditions and will prevail in prayer. But it cannot be too distinctly understood that *none others will*. What we commonly hear in prayer and conference meetings is not prevailing prayer. It is often astonishing and lamentable to witness the delusions that prevail on the subject. Who that has witnessed real revivals of religion has not been struck with the change that comes over the whole spirit and manner of the prayers of really revived Christians? I do not think I ever could have been converted if I had not discovered the solution to the question, Why is it that so much that is called prayer is not answered?

– 7 –
How to Win Souls

How to Win Souls

ake heed unto thyself, and unto the doctrine;
continue in them: for in doing this thou shalt
both save thyself, and them that hear thee"
(1 Timothy 4:16).

I wish to suggest to my younger brothers in the
ministry some thoughts on the philosophy of
preaching the Gospel in a way that will bring about
the salvation of souls. They are the result of much
study, much prayer for divine teaching, and a practical experience of many years.

I understand the verse at the beginning of this
chapter to relate to the matter, order, and manner
of preaching.

The problem is, How can we win souls wholly
to Christ? Certainly we must win them away from
themselves. Here, then, are several points to consider in winning souls.

People Are in Rebellion against God

Of course, people are free moral agents—rational, accountable. They are in rebellion against
God, wholly alienated, intensely prejudiced, and
committed against Him. They are committed to
self-gratification as their purpose for living.

This committed state is moral depravity, the fountain of sin within them, from which flows by a natural law all their sinful ways. This committed, voluntary state is their wicked heart. It is this that needs a radical change.

God is infinitely benevolent, and unconverted sinners are supremely selfish, so that they are radically opposed to God. Their commitment to the gratification of their appetites and inclinations is known in Bible language as *"the carnal mind"* or the minding of the flesh, which is *"enmity against God"* (Romans 8:7).

Enmity against God Is Overcome by the Word

This enmity is voluntary, and must be overcome, if at all, by the Word of God, made effective by the teaching of the Holy Spirit.

The Gospel is adapted to this end; and, when it is wisely presented, we may confidently expect the effective cooperation of the Holy Spirit. This assurance is implied in our commission, *"Go ye therefore, and teach all nations....And, lo, I am with you alway, even unto the end of the world"* (Matthew 28:19–20).

If we are unwise, illogical, and out of all natural order in presenting the Gospel, we have no right to expect divine cooperation.

God Works through and with Natural Laws

In winning souls, as in everything else, God works through and in accordance with natural laws. Hence, if we would win souls, we must wisely follow natural laws. We must present the necessary truths and do so in an order adapted to the natural laws of mind, of thought, and mental action. A false mental philosophy will greatly mislead us, and we will often be found ignorantly working against the Holy Spirit.

The Knowledge of Sin Comes from the Law

Sinners must be convicted of their enmity. They do not know God; consequently, they are often ignorant of the opposition of their hearts to Him. *"By the law is the knowledge of sin"* (Romans 3:20), because by the law the sinner acquires his first true idea of God. By the law, he first learns that God is perfectly benevolent and in-

> Sinners are often unaware that their hearts are opposed to God.

finitely opposed to all selfishness. This law, then, should be arrayed in all its majesty against the selfishness and enmity of the sinner. This law carries irresistible conviction of its righteousness, and no moral agent can doubt it.

All men know that they have sinned, but not all are convicted of the guilt and deserved punishment of sin. Many are careless and do not feel the burden of sin or the horrors and terrors of remorse. They do not have a sense of condemnation or of being lost. But without this, they cannot understand or appreciate the gospel method of salvation. One cannot intelligently and heartily ask or accept a pardon until he sees the justice of his condemnation.

It is absurd to suppose that a careless sinner, not convicted of sin, can intelligently and thankfully accept the gospel offer of pardon. He must first accept the righteousness of God in his condemnation. Conversion to Christ is a change in the mind. Hence, the conviction of deserved punishment must precede the acceptance of mercy; for without this conviction, the soul does not understand its need of mercy and, of course, the offer is rejected. The Gospel is no glad tidings to the careless sinner who is not convicted of sin.

The spirituality of the law should be unsparingly applied to the conscience until the sinner's self-righteousness is annihilated, and he stands speechless and self-condemned before a holy God.

In some men, this conviction is already ripe, and the preacher may at once present Christ, with the hope of His being accepted. But at ordinary times, such cases are rare. The great mass of sinners are careless, not convicted. Therefore, to assume that they are convicted and ready to receive Christ, and to immediately urge them to accept Him, is to begin at the wrong end of our work. They will not understand our teaching. And such a course will be found to have been a mistaken one, even if the results seem good and the sinner makes a profession. The sinner may obtain a hope under such teaching; but, unless the Holy Spirit supplies something that the preacher has failed to do, it will be found to be a false one. All the essential links of truth must be supplied.

The law does its work—it annihilates the sinner's self-righteousness and shows him that mercy is his only hope. Then, he should be made to understand that it is morally impossible for a just

God not to execute a penalty when the law has been broken.

At this point, the sinner should be made to understand that he cannot assume that because God is benevolent, He will forgive him. For unless public justice can be satisfied, the law of universal benevolence forbids the forgiveness of sin. If public justice is not regarded in the exercise of mercy, the good of the public is sacrificed to that of the individual. God will never do this. This teaching will give the sinner no choice but to look for some offering to public justice.

Present the Atonement as a Revealed Fact

Next, present the Atonement to the sinner as a revealed fact and point to Christ alone as his own sin offering. Stress the revealed fact that God has accepted the death of Christ as a substitute for the sinner's death, and that this is to be received upon the testimony of God.

Since the sinner is already crushed into contrition by the convicting power of the law, the revelation of the love of God manifested in the death of Christ will naturally produce great self-loathing. It will produce that godly sorrow that needs *"not to be repented of"* (2 Corinthians 7:10). Under this evidence, the sinner can never forgive himself. God is holy and glorious, while the sinner must be saved by sovereign grace. This teaching may be more or less formal, as the souls you address are more or less thoughtful, intelligent, and able to understand.

It was not by accident that the dispensation of law preceded the dispensation of grace, but is in the natural order of things and in accordance with established mental laws. Evermore, the law must prepare the way for the Gospel. To overlook this point in instructing souls is almost certain to result in false hope and in the introduction of a false standard of Christian experience; it will also fill the church with false converts. Time will make this plain.

Give People a Personal Interest in the Gospel

The truth should be preached to the people present and so personally applied as to compel everyone to feel that you mean *him* or *her.* It has often been said of a certain preacher, "He does not preach, but explains clearly what other people preach, and seems to be talking directly to *me.*"

This course will rivet attention and cause your hearers to forget about the length of your sermon. They will tire if they feel no personal interest in what you say. Getting their individual interest in what you are saying is an indispensable condition of their being saved. And when their individual interest is thus awakened and held fast to your subject, they will seldom complain of the length of your sermon. In nearly all cases, if the people complain of the length of our sermons, it is because we fail to interest them personally in what we have to say.

People need to know that the truth applies to them personally.

If we fail to interest them personally, it is either because we do not address them personally, because we lack fervency and earnestness, because we lack clearness and force, or because we lack something else that we ought to possess. To make them feel that we and that God mean *them* is indispensable.

Use Common Sense and Spiritual Wisdom

Do not think that earnest piety alone can make you successful in winning souls. This is only one condition of success. There must be common sense; there must be spiritual wisdom in adapting means to the end. Matter and manner and order and time and place all need to be wisely adjusted to the end that we have in view.

God may sometimes convert souls through the efforts of men who are not spiritually minded, when they possess that natural discernment that enables them to use the proper means; but the Bible tells us these cases are rare. Yet, without using discernment and the proper means, even a spiritual mind will fail to win souls to Christ.

Instruct according to Intelligence

Souls need instruction in accordance with the measure of their intelligence. A few simple truths, when wisely applied and illuminated by the Holy Spirit, will convert children to Christ. I say wisely applied, for they, too, are sinners and need the application of the law, as a schoolmaster, to bring them to Christ, so that they may be justified by faith (Galatians 3:24). If the preparatory law work has been omitted, and Christ has not been embraced as a Savior from sin and condemnation, one cannot be saved. It will sooner or later be known that supposed conversions to Christ are false where these two things have been omitted.

Educated and cultured sinners, who are, perhaps as a result, skeptical and not convicted in their hearts, need a much more extensive and thorough explanation of truth. Professional men need the gospel net to be thrown completely around them, with no break through which they can escape; and, when thus dealt with, they are all the more sure to be converted in proportion to their real intelligence. I have found that a course of lectures addressed to lawyers and adapted to their habits of thought and reasoning is most likely to result in their conversion.

To be successful in winning souls, we need to be observant—to study individual character, and to stress the facts of experience, observation, and revelation to the consciences of all classes.

Explain Spiritual Terms

Be sure to explain the terms you use. Before I was converted, I failed to hear the terms *repentance, faith, regeneration,* and *conversion* intelligibly explained. Repentance was described as a feeling. Faith was represented as an intellectual act or state and not as a voluntary act of trust. Regeneration was represented as some physical change in the nature, produced by the direct power of the Holy Spirit. It was not explained that it is a voluntary change of the ultimate preference of the soul, produced by the spiritual illumination of the Holy Spirit. Conversion, also, was represented as being so completely the work of the Holy Spirit that the fact that it is the sinner's own act, under the persuasions of the Holy Spirit, was covered up.

Urge the fact that repentance involves the voluntary and actual renunciation of all sin, that it is a radical change of mind toward God.

Also emphasize the fact that saving faith is heart-trust in Christ, that it works by love, that it purifies the heart and overcomes the world. No faith is saving that does not have these attributes.

Stress Mental Efforts and Acts of the Will

The sinner is required to put forth certain mental efforts. He needs to understand what these are. Errors in intellectual reasoning only embarrass and may fatally deceive the inquiring soul. Sinners are often put on a wrong track. They are put under a strain to *feel* instead of putting forth the required acts of *will*. Before my conversion, I never received from man any intelligible idea of the mental acts that God required of me.

Be Thorough

The deceitfulness of sin renders the inquiring soul exceedingly exposed to delusion; therefore, it is necessary for teachers to beat every bush and to search out every nook and corner where a soul can find a false refuge. Be so thorough and discriminating that it will be impossible, as far as you can make it, for the inquirer to entertain a false hope.

Do not fear to be thorough. Do not through false pity dress a wound when the probe is needed.

Do not fear that you will discourage the convicted sinner and turn him back by searching him out to the bottom. If the Holy Spirit is dealing with him, the more you search and probe, the more impossible it will be for the soul to turn back or rest in sin.

If you want to save the soul, do not spare a right hand or right eye or any favorite idol, but see to it that every form of sin is given up. (See Matthew 5:29–30.) Insist on full confession of wrong to all that have a right to confession. Insist on full restitution, so far as possible, to all injured parties. Do not fall short of the explicit teaching of Christ on this subject. Whoever the sinner may be, let him distinctly understand that unless he forsakes all that he has, he cannot be a disciple of Christ. Insist on entire and total consecration to God of all powers of body and mind, and of all property, possessions, character, and influence. Insist on total abandonment to God of all ownership of self, or anything else, as a condition of being accepted.

From first to last, the sinner is to find his whole salvation in Christ.

Understand for yourself, and, if possible, make the sinner understand, that nothing short of these things is involved in true faith or true repentance, and that true consecration involves them all.

Let the Sinner Know He is Dealing with the Personal Christ

Keep constantly before the sinner's mind that it is the personal Christ with whom he is dealing.

It is God in Christ seeking his reconciliation to Himself (2 Corinthians 5:19). The condition of his reconciliation is that he gives up his will and his whole being to God—that *"not an hoof be left behind"* (Exodus 10:26).

Assure him that *"God hath given to* [him] *eternal life, and this life is in his Son"* (1 John 5:11), and that *"Christ...is made unto* [him] *wisdom, and righteousness, and sanctification, and redemption"* (1 Corinthians 1:30). From first to last, he is to find his whole salvation in Christ.

Instruct People in the Basic Precepts of the Christian Life

When you are satisfied that the soul intelligently receives all this doctrine, and the Christ therein revealed, instruct him in the basic precepts of the Christian life. Warn him that sin consists in carnal-mindedness, in *"fulfilling the desires of the flesh and of the mind"* (Ephesians 2:3). Challenge him with the truth that *"to be spiritually minded is life and peace"* (Romans 8:6).

Instruct him about the indwelling Holy Spirit, by whose fervency and power all victory against Satan comes. And exhort him to *"run with patience the race that is set before* [him], *looking unto Jesus the author and finisher of* [his] *faith"* (Hebrews 12:1–2)—that he may *"adorn the doctrine of God our Saviour in all things"* (Titus 2:10), be *"approved in Christ"* (Romans 16:10), and ultimately gain the victor's crown.

– 8 –
Preacher, Save Thyself

– 8 –

Preacher, Save Thyself

Take heed unto thyself, and unto the doctrine; continue in them: for in doing this thou shalt both save thyself, and them that hear thee" (1 Timothy 4:16).

In this chapter, I am not going to preach to preachers and other Christians, but to suggest certain ways they can save themselves from sorrow and failure and from the disapproval and reproof of Him who has called them to His service:

♦ See that you are constrained by love to preach the Gospel, as Christ was to provide a Gospel.

♦ See that you have the special infusion of power from on high, by the baptism of the Holy Spirit.

♦ See that you have a heart and not merely a head call to undertake the preaching of the Gospel. By this, I mean, be heartily and most intensely inclined to seek the salvation of souls as the great work of life, and do not undertake what you have no heart to do.

♦ Constantly maintain a close walk with God.

♦ Make the Bible your Book of books. Study it much, upon your knees, waiting for divine light.

- ◆ Beware of leaning on Bible commentaries. Consult them when convenient, but judge for yourself in the light of the Holy Spirit.
- ◆ Keep yourself pure—in will, in thought, in feeling, in word, and in action.
- ◆ Contemplate much the guilt and danger of sinners so that your zeal for their salvation may be intensified.
- ◆ Deeply ponder and dwell much on the boundless love and compassion of Christ for sinners.
- ◆ So love them yourself as to be willing to die for them.
- ◆ Give your most intense thought to the study of ways and means by which you may save them. Make this the great and intense study of your life.
- ◆ Refuse to be diverted from this work. Guard against every temptation that would abate your interest in it.
- ◆ Believe the promise of Christ that He is with you in this work always and everywhere, to give you all the help you need (Matthew 28:20).
- ◆ *"He that winneth souls is wise"* (Proverbs 11:30). *"If any of you lack wisdom, let him ask of God, that giveth to all men liberally, and upbraideth not; and it shall be given him. But let him ask in faith"* (James 1:5–6). Remember, therefore, that you are bound to have the wisdom that will win souls to Christ.
- ◆ Being called of God to the work, make your calling your constant ground with God for all that you need for the accomplishment of the work.

- Be diligent and active, *"in season,* [and] *out of season"* (2 Timothy 4:2).
- Converse much with all classes of your hearers on the question of their salvation so that you may understand their opinions, errors, and needs. Ascertain their prejudices, ignorance, temper, habits, and whatever you need to know to adapt your instruction to their necessities.
- See that your own habits are in all respects correct, that you are temperate in all things— free from the stain or smell of tobacco, alcohol, drugs, or anything of which you have reason to be ashamed and that may cause others to stumble.
- Do not be frivolous, but *"set the LORD always before* [you]" (Psalm 16:8).
- Bridle your tongue, and do not be given to idle and unprofitable conversation.
- Always let your people see that you are in solemn earnest with them, both in the pulpit and out of it. Do not let your daily contacts with them nullify your serious teaching on Sunday.
- Resolve to know nothing among your people *"save Jesus Christ, and him crucified"* (1 Corinthians 2:2). Let them understand that as an ambassador of Christ, your business with them relates wholly to the salvation of their souls.
- Be sure to teach them by example, not just by precept. Practice yourself what you preach.
- Be especially on guard in your contacts with women, to raise no thought or suspicion of the least impurity in yourself.
- Guard your weak points. If you naturally tend to festivity and joking, watch against occasions for failure in this direction. If you are naturally

somber and unsocial, guard against sullenness and unsociability.

♦ Avoid all affectation and sham in all things. Be what you profess to be, and you will have no temptation to make believe. Let simplicity, sincerity, and Christian propriety stamp your whole life.

♦ Spend much time every day and night in prayer and direct communion with God. This will empower you to win souls. No amount of learning and study can compensate for the loss of this communion. If you fail to maintain communion with God, you are *weak...as another man* (Judges 16:11).

♦ Beware of the error that there are no means of regeneration and, consequently, no connection between means and ends in the regeneration of souls.

♦ Understand that conversion is a moral and therefore a voluntary change.

♦ Understand that the Gospel is adapted to change the hearts of men. In a wise presentation of it, you may expect the effective cooperation of the Holy Spirit.

♦ In the selection and treatment of your texts, always acquire the direct teaching of the Holy Spirit.

♦ Let all your sermons be heart and not merely head sermons. Preach from experience and not from hearsay or from mere reading and study.

♦ Always present the subject that the Holy Spirit lays upon your heart for the occasion. Seize the points presented by the Holy Spirit to your own mind, and present them with the greatest possible directness to your congregation.

- Be full of prayer whenever you attempt to preach, and go from your place of prayer to your pulpit with the inward groanings of the Spirit pressing for utterance at your lips.

- Fill your mind completely with your subject so that it will press for utterance; then open your mouth, and let it come forth like a torrent.

- See that *"the fear of man* [that] *bringeth a snare"* (Proverbs 29:25) is not upon you. Let your people understand that you fear God too much to be afraid of them. Never let the question of your popularity with your people influence your preaching.

- Never let the question of salary deter you from *"declaring...the whole counsel of God"* (Acts 20:27 RV), *"whether they will hear, or whether they will forbear"* (Ezekiel 2:5). Do not let them for one moment suppose that you can be influenced in your preaching by any considerations of salary, whether more, or less, or none at all.

- Do not compromise, or you may lose the confidence of your people and fail to save them. They cannot thoroughly respect you as an ambassador of Christ if they see that you are afraid to do your duty.

- Be sure to commend yourself *"to every man's conscience in the sight of God"* (2 Corinthians 4:2).

- Be *"not greedy of filthy lucre"* (1 Timothy 3:3).

- Avoid every appearance of vanity.

- So live and labor as to compel your people to respect your sincerity and your spiritual wisdom.

- Do not make the impression that you are fond of good dinners and like to be invited out to dine, for this will be a snare to you and a stumbling block to them.

♦ Discipline your body, so that, after preaching to others, you yourself will not be a castaway. (See 1 Corinthians 9:27.)

♦ *"Watch for* [their] *souls, as* [one] *that must give account* [to God]" (Hebrews 13:17).

♦ Be a diligent student, and thoroughly instruct your people in all that is essential to their salvation.

♦ Never flatter the rich.

♦ Be especially attentive to the needs and the instruction of the poor.

♦ Do not allow yourself to be bribed into a compromise with sin by givers of donations.

♦ Do not allow yourself to be publicly treated as a beggar, or you will be despised by a large class of your hearers.

♦ Repel people's attempts to keep you from speaking out against whatever is extravagant, wrong, or injurious among your people.

♦ Maintain your pastoral integrity and independence, lest you sear your conscience, quench the Holy Spirit, forfeit the confidence of your people, and lose the favor of God.

♦ Be an example to the flock, and let your life illustrate your teaching. Remember that your actions and spirit will teach even more impressively than your sermons.

♦ If you preach that men should offer to God and their neighbor a love-service, see that you do this yourself. Avoid all that tends to the belief that you are working for pay.

♦ Give to your people a love-service. Encourage them to render to you not a money reward equivalent to your labor but a love reward that will refresh both you and them.

♦ Repel every proposal to get money for you or for church purposes that will naturally disgust and will excite the contempt of worldly but thoughtful men.

♦ Resist the introduction of parties, amusing lectures, and extravagant socials, especially at those seasons most favorable for united efforts to convert souls to Christ. Be sure, the Devil will try to head you off in this direction. When you are praying and planning for a revival of God's work, some of your worldly church members will invite you to a party. Do not go, or you are in for a cycle of them, which will defeat your prayers.

♦ Do not be deceived. Your spiritual power with your people will never be increased by accepting invitations at such times. If it is a good time to have parties because the people have leisure, it is also a good time for religious meetings, and your influence should be used to draw the people to church.

♦ See that you personally know and daily live upon Christ.

- 9 -
INNOCENT AMUSEMENTS

- 9 -

INNOCENT AMUSEMENTS

We hear much said and read much these days about indulging in innocent amusements. I heard a minister some time ago, in addressing a large company of young people, say that he had spent much time devising innocent amusements for the young. Within the past few years, I have read several sermons and numerous articles pleading for more amusements than have been customary with religious people. I wish to suggest a few thoughts on this subject—first, what are not, and, second, what are *innocent* amusements. This is a question of morals.

All intelligent acts of a moral agent must be either right or wrong. Nothing is innocent in a moral agent that is not in accordance with the law and Gospel of God.

The moral character of any and every act of a moral agent resides in the motive or the ultimate reason for the act. This I take to be self-evident and universally admitted.

Now, what is the rule of judgment in this case? How are we to decide whether any given act of amusement is right or wrong, innocent or sinful?

How to Know If an Amusement is Right or Wrong

I answer that it is by three ways. First, by the moral law, *"Thou shalt love the Lord thy God with all thy heart, and...thy neighbour as thyself"* (Matthew 22:37, 39). No intelligent act of a moral agent is innocent or right unless it proceeds from and is an expression of supreme love to God and equal love to man—in other words, unless it is benevolent. Second, we decide if an amusement is innocent by the Gospel. This requires the same:

> A moral agent must have a higher ultimate motive than gratifying the appetites.

"Whether therefore ye eat, or drink, or whatsoever ye do, do all to the glory of God" (1 Corinthians 10:31). *"Do all in the name of the Lord Jesus"* (Colossians 3:17). Third, we decide by right reason, which affirms the same thing.

Now, in the light of this rule, it is plain that it is not innocent to engage in amusements merely to gratify the desire for amusement. We may not innocently eat or drink to gratify the desire for food or drink. To eat or drink to gratify the appetite is innocent enough in a mere animal, but in a moral agent, it is a sin. A moral agent is obligated to have a higher ultimate motive—to eat and drink that he may be strong and healthy for the service of God. God has made eating and drinking pleasant to us, but this pleasure ought not to be our ultimate reason for eating and drinking.

So, amusements are pleasant, but this does not justify us in seeking amusements to gratify desire. Mere animals may do this innocently because they are incapable of any higher motive, but moral agents are under a higher law and are obligated to have another and a higher aim than merely to gratify the desire for amusements. Therefore, no amusement is innocent that is engaged in for the pleasure of the amusement, any more than it would be innocent to eat and drink for the pleasure of it.

Again, no amusement is innocent that is engaged in merely because we need amusements. We need food and drink, but this does not justify us in eating and drinking simply because we need it. The law of God does not say to seek whatever you need because you need it, but to do all from love to God and man. A wicked man might eat and drink selfishly—that is, to make his body strong to execute his selfish plans—and this eating and drinking would be sin, even though he needed food and drink.

Nothing is innocent unless it proceeds from supreme love to God and equal love to man, unless the supreme and ultimate motive is to please and honor God. In other words, to be innocent, any amusement must be engaged in because it is believed to be, at the time, most pleasing to God. It must be intended to be a service rendered to Him— a service that, on the whole, will honor Him more than anything else that we can engage in for the time being. I take this to be self-evident. What then?

None but Benevolent Amusements Can Be Innocent

It follows that none but benevolent amusements can be innocent. Fishing and shooting for amusement are not innocent. We may fish and hunt for the same reason that we are allowed to eat and drink—for nourishment, that we may be strong in the service of God. We may hunt to destroy noxious animals, for the glory of God and the interests of His kingdom; but fishing and hunting to gratify a passion for these sports is not innocent.

Amusements That Waste Time

Again, no amusement can be innocent that involves the squandering of precious time that might be better employed to the glory of God and the good of man. Life is short. Time is precious. We have but one life to live. Much is to be done. The world is in darkness. A world of sinners are to be enlightened and, if possible, saved. We are required to work while the day lasts. Our commission and work require haste. No time is to be lost. If our hearts are right, our work is pleasant. If rightly performed, it gives the highest enjoyment and is itself the highest amusement. No turning aside for amusement can be innocent that involves any unnecessary loss of time. No man who realizes the greatness of the work to be done, and loves to do it, can turn aside for any amusement involving an unnecessary waste of time.

Amusements That Waste Money

Again, no amusement can be innocent that involves an unnecessary expenditure of the Lord's money. All our time and all our money are the

Lord's. We are the Lord's. We may innocently use both time and money to promote the Lord's interests and the highest interests of man, which are the Lord's interests. But we may not innocently use either for our own pleasure and gratification. Expensive journeys for our own pleasure and amusement, and not undertaken with a single eye to the glory of God, are not innocent amusements but sinful.

Sinners and Amusements

Again, in the light of the above rule of judgment, we see that no form of amusement is lawful for an unsaved sinner. Nothing in him is innocent. While he remains unrepentant and unbelieving, and does not love God and his neighbor according to God's command, there is for him no innocent activity or amusement; all is sin.

Regarding this, I fear that many are acting under a great delusion. The loose manner in which this subject is viewed by many professing Christians, and even ministers, is surprising and alarming. Some time ago, in a sermon, I remarked that there were no lawful activities or innocent amusements for sinners. An aged clergyman who was present said, after the service, that it was ridiculous to hold that nothing is lawful or innocent in an unrepentant sinner. I replied, "I thought you were orthodox. Do you not believe in the universal necessity of regeneration by the Holy Spirit?"

He replied, "Yes."

I added, "Do you believe that an unregenerate soul does anything acceptable to God? Before his

101

heart is changed, does he ever act from a motive that God can accept, in anything whatever? Is he not totally depraved, in the sense that his heart is all wrong, and therefore his actions must be all wrong?" He appeared embarrassed, saw the point, and quietly left.

Whatever is lawful in a moral agent or according to the law of God is right. If anyone is to do anything lawfully, he must do it from supreme love to God and equal love to his neighbor. And if he were doing it from supreme love, he would not be an unrepentant sinner but a Christian. It is simply absurd and a contradiction to say that an unrepentant soul does, says, or omits anything with a right heart. If he is unrepentant, his ultimate motive must necessarily be wrong. Consequently, nothing in him is innocent, but all must be sinful.

> Whatever is lawful in a moral agent or according to the law of God is right.

What Is an Innocent Amusement?

What, then, is an innocent amusement? It must be that and only that which not only might be, but actually *is*, engaged in with a single eye to God's glory and the interests of His kingdom. If this is not the ultimate and supreme design, it is not an innocent but a sinful amusement.

Now, many people are deluded about this point, I fear. When speaking of amusements, they say, "What harm is there in them?" In answering to themselves and others this question, they do not penetrate to the bottom of it. If, on the surface, they see nothing contrary to morality, they judge that the amusement is innocent. They fail to look for the supreme and ultimate motive, which will tell them if the act is innocent or sinful. But apart from the motive, no course of action is either innocent or sinful, any more than the motions of a machine or the acts of a mere animal are innocent or sinful. No act or course of action should, therefore, be judged innocent or sinful without determining the supreme motive of the person who acts.

To teach, either directly or by implication, that any amusement of an unrepentant sinner or of a backslider is innocent is to teach a gross and ruinous heresy. Parents should remember this in regard to the amusements of their unsaved children. Sunday school teachers and superintendents who are planning amusements for their Sunday schools should remember this. Preachers who spend their time in planning amusements for the young, who lead their flocks to picnics and pleasure excursions, and who justify various games, should bear something in mind. They should certainly remember that unless they are in a holy state of heart, and do all these things from supreme love to God and the highest intention to glorify God, these ways of spending time are by no means innocent but highly criminal. Those who teach people to walk in these ways are simply directing the channels in which their depravity will run.

Always remember that unless these things are indulged in from supreme love to God and designed to glorify Him—unless they are, in fact, engaged in with a single eye to the glory of God—they are not innocent but sinful amusements. I must say again, and, if possible, still more emphatically, that it is not enough that they might be engaged in as the best way, for the time being, to honor and please God. But they must be actually engaged in from supreme love to God, with the ultimate design to glorify Him.

If such, then, is the true doctrine of innocent amusements, let no unrepentant sinner and no backslidden Christian suppose for a moment that he can engage in any innocent amusement. The aged minister to whom I have referred and many others seem to believe that unrepentant sinners or backsliders can and do engage in innocent amusements. But if this were true, the very engaging in such amusements, being lawfully right and innocent, would involve a change of heart in the unsaved and a return to God in the backslider.

No amusement is lawful unless it is engaged in as a love-service rendered to God and designed to please and glorify Him. It must be not only a love-service, but also, in the judgment of the one who gives it, the best service he can give to God for the time being. It must be a service that will be more pleasing to Him and more useful to His kingdom than any other that can be engaged in at the time. Let these facts be borne in mind when the question of engaging in amusements comes up for decision. And remember, the question in all such cases is not, What harm is there in this proposed amusement? but, What good can it do? Is it the best way in which I can spend my time? Will it be more pleasing to God and more for the interests of His kingdom than anything else at present possible to me? If not, it is not an innocent amusement, and I cannot engage in it without sin.

The question often arises, Are we never to seek such amusements? My answer is that it is our privilege and our duty to live above a desire for such things. All of that class of desires should be subdued by living close to God. We should be living so much in the light of God and having so deep a communion with Him that we will not feel the need of worldly excitements, sports, pastimes, and entertainments for enjoyment. If a Christian avails himself of his privilege of communion with God, he will naturally and by an instinct of his new nature repel solicitation to go after worldly amusements. To him, such pastimes will appear low, unsatisfactory, and even repulsive. If he is of a heavenly mind, as he ought to be, he will feel as if he could not afford to come down and seek enjoyment in worldly amusements.

Surely, a Christian must be fallen from his first love, he must have turned back into the world, before he can feel the necessity or have the desire of seeking enjoyment in worldly sports and pastimes. A spiritual mind cannot seek enjoyment in worldly society. To such a mind, that society is necessarily repulsive. Worldly society is insincere, hollow, and, to a great extent, a sham. What relish can a spiritual mind have for the gossip of a worldly party of pleasure? None whatever. To a mind in communion with God, their worldly spirit and ways, their conversation and folly, are repulsive. Their ways are even painful, since they are so strongly suggestive of the downward tendency of their souls and of the destiny that awaits them.

I have had so marked an experience of both sides of this question that I think I cannot be mistaken. Probably few people enjoy worldly pleasure more intensely than I did before I was converted; but my conversion, and the spiritual baptism that immediately followed it, completely extinguished all desire for worldly sports and amusements. I was lifted at once into an entirely different plane of life and another kind of enjoyment. From that hour to the present, the mode of life, pastimes, sports, amusements, and worldly ways that so much delighted me before have failed to interest me. Moreover, I have had a strong aversion to them. I have never felt them necessary to, or even compatible with, a truly rational enjoyment. I do not speak boastfully; however, for the honor of Christ and His religion, I must say that my Christian life has been a happy one. I have found as much enjoyment as is probably best for men to have in one life, and never for an hour have I had the desire to turn back and seek enjoyment from anything the world can give.

> Professing Christians should maintain a life consistent with their profession.

But some may ask, "Suppose we do not find sufficient enjoyment in religion, and we really desire to go after worldly amusements. If we have the disposition, is it not as well to gratify it?" They may also ask, "Is there any more sin in seeking amusements than in entertaining a longing for them?" I reply that a longing for them should never be entertained. It is the privilege and therefore the duty of everyone to rise, through grace, above a hungering and thirsting for Egypt's pots of meat (see Exodus 16:3), worldly pastimes, and time-wasting amusements. The indulgence of such longings is not innocent. One should not ask whether the longing should be gratified, but whether it should not be displaced by a longing for the glory of God and His kingdom.

Professed Christians are obligated to maintain a life consistent with their profession. For the honor of religion, they ought to deny worldly lusts, and not, by seeking to gratify them, give occasion to the world to scoff and say that Christians love the world as well as they do. If professors of Christ are backslidden in heart and entertain a longing for worldly sports and amusements, they are bound by duty and decency to abstain from all outward manifestation of such inward lustings.

Some have maintained that we should conform to the ways of the world somewhat—at least enough to show that we can enjoy the world and religion too. They have maintained that we make religion appear repulsive to unsaved souls by turning our backs on what they call their innocent amusements. But we should represent religion as it really is—as living above the world, as consisting in a heavenly mind, as that which gives an enjoyment so spiritual and heavenly as to render the low pursuits and joys of worldly men disagreeable and repulsive.

It is a sad stumbling block to the unsaved to see professed Christians seeking pleasure or happiness from this world. Such seeking is a misrepresentation of the religion of Jesus. It misleads, bewilders, and confounds the observing outsider. If he ever reads his Bible, he cannot help but wonder that souls who are born of God and have communion with Him should have any relish for worldly ways and pleasures. The fact is that thoughtful sinners have little or no confidence in the class of professing Christians who seek enjoyment from this world. They may profess to have, and may loosely think of such as being liberal and good Christians. They may flatter them and commend their religion as being the opposite of fanaticism and bigotry, and as being such a religion as they like to see, but there is no real sincerity in what they are saying.

In my early Christian life, I heard a Methodist bishop from the South report a case that made a deep impression on my mind. He said there was in his neighborhood a slaveholder, a gentleman of fortune, who was a jovial and agreeable man and spent much time in various field sports and amusements. He used to associate much with his pastor, often inviting him to dinner and to accompany him in his sports and pleasure-seeking excursions. The minister cheerfully complied with these requests, and a friendship grew up between the pastor and his parishioner that continued until the last sickness of this jovial and wealthy man.

When the wife of this worldling was apprised that her husband would soon die, she was much alarmed for his soul and tenderly asked if she should call their minister to converse and pray with him. He feelingly replied, "No, my dear. He is not the man for me to see now. He was my companion, as you know, in worldly sports and pleasure-seeking; he loved good dinners and a merry time. I then enjoyed his society and found him a pleasant companion. But I see now that I never had any confidence in his piety and have now no confidence in the efficacy of his prayers. I am now a dying man and need the instruction and prayers of somebody who can prevail with God. We have been much together, but our pastor has never been in earnest with me about the salvation of my soul, and he is not the man to help me now."

The wife was greatly affected and said, "What should I do, then?"

He replied, "My coachman, Tom, is a pious man. I have confidence in his prayers. I have often overheard him pray when about the barn or stables, and his prayers have always struck me as being quite sincere and earnest. I never heard any foolishness from him. He has always been honest and earnest as a Christian man. Call him."

Tom was called, and he came to the door, dropping his hat and looking tenderly and compassionately at his dying master. The dying man put forth his hand, saying, "Come here, Tom. Take my hand. Tom, can you pray for your dying master?" Tom poured out his soul in earnest prayer.

I cannot remember the name of this bishop, it was so long ago, but the story I well remember as an illustration of the mistake into which many professing Christians and some ministers fall. The mistake is that we suppose we recommend religion to the unsaved by mingling with them in their pleasures and running after their amusements. I have seen many illustrations of this mistake.

Christians should live so far above the world as not to need or seek its pleasures, and thus they will recommend religion to the world as a source of the highest and purest happiness. The peaceful look, the joyful countenance, and the spiritual serenity and cheerfulness of a living Christian recommend religion to the unsaved. Their satisfaction in God, their holy joy, and their living above and shunning the ways and amusements of the world impress the unsaved with a sense of the necessity and desirableness of a Christian life. But let no man think he will gain a really Christian influence over another by showing a sympathy with his worldly aspirations.

Now, is this rule a yoke of bondage? I am not surprised that it has created in some minds a great disturbance. The pleasure-loving and pleasure-seeking members of the church regard the rule as impracticable, as a straitjacket, as a bondage. But to whom is it a straitjacket and a bondage? To whom is it impracticable? Surely, it is not and cannot be to any who love God with all their hearts and their neighbors as themselves. It certainly cannot be so regarded by a real Christian, for all real Christians love God supremely. Their own interests and their own pleasure are regarded as nothing as compared with the interests and good pleasure of God. They, therefore, cannot seek amusements unless they believe themselves called of God to do so.

> Christians find their highest enjoyment and their truest pleasure in pleasing God.

By a law of our nature, we seek to please those whom we supremely love. Also, by a law of our nature, we find our highest happiness in pleasing those whom we supremely love. We supremely please ourselves when we seek not to please ourselves at all but to please the object of our supreme affection. Therefore, Christians find their highest enjoyment and their truest pleasure in pleasing God and in seeking the good of their fellowmen. And they enjoy this service all the more because enjoyment is not what they seek but what they inevitably experience by a law of their nature.

There Is No Comparable Enjoyment to Doing God's Will

This is a fact of Christian consciousness. The highest and purest of all amusements is found in doing the will of God. Mere worldly amusements are cold and insipid and not worthy of naming in comparison to the enjoyment we find in doing the will of God. To one who loves God supremely, it is natural to seek amusements, and everything else that we seek, with supreme reference to the glory of God. Why, then, should this rule be regarded as too strict, as placing the standard too high, and as being a straitjacket and a bondage? How, then, are we to understand those who plead so much for worldly amusements?

From what I have heard and read on this subject within the last few years, I have gathered that these pleaders for amusements have thought that there was more enjoyment to be gained from these amusements than from the service of God. They remind me of a sentence that I used to have to copy when I was a schoolboy: "All work and no play makes Jack a dull boy." They seem to assume that the service of God is work in the sense of being a task and a burden. They think that to labor and pray and preach to win souls to Christ is so wearisome, not to say irksome, that we need a good many play days. They assume that the love of Christ is not satisfactory. They think that we must have to resort to worldly amusements frequently to make life tolerable.

On one occasion, Christ said to His disciples, *"Come...apart...and rest a while"* (Mark 6:31). This is not surprising when we consider that they were often so thronged they did not have time to eat even their ordinary meals. But it was not amusement that they sought—simply rest from their labors of love, in which labors they must have had the greatest enjoyment.

I often ask myself, "What can it mean that so many of our highly fed and most popular preachers are pleading so much for amusements?" They seem to be leading the church in a direction where she is in the most danger. It is no wonder that church men and women are easily led in that direction, for such teaching agrees exactly with the innumerable temptations to worldliness that bombard the church. The Bible is replete with instruction on this subject, which is the direct opposite of these pleas for worldly amusements. These teachers plead for fun, hilarity, jesting, plays, games, and such things as worldly minds love and enjoy; but the Bible exhorts to sobriety, heavenly mindedness, unceasing prayer, and a close and perpetual walk with God. The Bible everywhere assumes that all real enjoyment is found in this course of life, that all true peace of mind is found in communion with God and in giving our all to seek His glory. It exhorts us to watchfulness, and it informs us that we must give account in the Day of Judgment for every idle word (Matthew 12:36). It nowhere informs us that fun and hilarity are the source of rational enjoyment. If we wander about to seek amusements, the Bible nowhere promises a close walk with God or peace of mind and joy in the Holy Spirit.

And is not the teaching of the Bible on this subject in exact accordance with human experience? Do we need to have the pulpit turn advocate of worldly amusements? Is not human depravity strong enough in that direction without being stimulated by the voice of the preacher? Has the church worked so hard for God and souls, and are Christians so worn out with their exhausting efforts to pull sinners out of the fire, that they are in danger of becoming insane with religious fervor and need the pulpit and the press to join in urging them to seek amusements and have a little fun? What can it mean? Why, is it not true that nearly all our dangers are on this side? Is not human nature in its present state so strongly tending in these directions that we need to be on our guard and constantly to exhort the church *not* to be led away after amusements and fun, to the destruction of their souls?

But let us come back to the question, To whom is it a bondage to be required to have a single eye to the good pleasure and glory of God in all that we do? Who finds it hard to do so? Christ says, *"My yoke is easy, and my burden is light"* (Matthew 11:30). The requirement to do all for the glory of God is surely none other than the yoke of Christ. It is His expressed will. Who finds this a hard yoke and a heavy burden? It is not hard or heavy to a willing, loving mind.

What is required here is natural and inevitable to everyone who truly loves God and is truly devoted to the Savior. What is devotion to Jesus but a heart set on rendering Him a loving obedience in all things? What is Christian liberty but the privilege of doing what Christians most love to do—that is, in all things to fulfill the good pleasure of their blessed Lord? Turn aside from saving souls to seek amusements! As if there could be a higher and more divine pleasure than is found in laboring for the salvation of souls. There cannot be. There can be no higher enjoyment found in this world than is found in pulling souls out of the fire and bringing them to Christ. I am filled with amazement when I read and hear the appeals to the church to seek more worldly amusements. Do we need, or can we have, any fuller and higher satisfaction than is found in a close, serious, loving walk with God and cooperation with Him in fitting souls for heaven?

> Devotion to Jesus is a heart set on rendering Him a loving obedience in all things.

All that I hear said to encourage Christians to seek amusements appears to proceed from a worldly instead of a spiritual state of mind. Can it be possible that a soul in communion with God and, of course, yearning with compassion over dying men, struggling from day to day in agonizing prayer for their salvation, should entertain the thought of turning aside to seek amusement? Can a pastor in whose congregation are numbers of unsaved souls, and among whose membership are many worldly-minded professing Christians, turn aside and lead or accompany his church in a back-sliding movement to gain worldly pleasure? There are always enough in every church who are easily led astray in that direction.

But who are they that most readily fall in with such a movement? Who are ready to come to the front when a picnic, a worldly party, or other pleasure-seeking activities are proposed? Are they, in fact, the class that always attends prayer meetings, that are always in a revival state of mind? Do they belong to the class whose faces shine from day to day with the peace of God pervading their souls? Are they the Aarons and Hurs that hold up the hands of their pastor with continual and prevailing prayer? (See Exodus 17:10–12.) Are they spiritual members, whose homeland is in heaven and whose mind is not on earthly things? Who does not know that it is the worldly members in the congregation who are always ready for any movement in the direction of worldly pleasure or amusement, and that the truly spiritual, prayerful, heavenly-minded members are shy of all such movements? They are not led into them without urging, and they weep in secret places when they see their pastor giving encouragement to what is likely to be so great a stumbling block to both the church and the world.

* * * * *

President Finney of Oberlin College, in forwarding his revision of the above for publication, accompanied it with a note, in which he said,

The previous pages contain a condensation of three short articles that I published in the *Independent*. I recollect that the editor of the *Advance* and one of the editors of the *Independent*—both of whom had published what I regard as very loose views, approving and recommending the worldly amusements of Christians—criticized those articles with a severity that seemed to indicate that they were offended by them. They so far perverted them as to assert that they taught asceticism and the prohibition of rest, recreation, and all amusements. I regard the doctrine of what I have written as strictly biblical and true. But, to avoid all such unjust inferences and quibbles, add the following lines:

Let no one say that the doctrine here presented prohibits all rest, recreation, and amusement whatever. It does not. It freely allows for all rest, recreation, and amusement that is regarded by the person who resorts to it as means of securing health and vigor of body and mind with which to promote the cause of God. It only insists, as the Bible does, that *"whether therefore* [we] *eat, or drink"* (1 Corinthians 10:31), rest, recreate, or amuse ourselves, all must be done as a service rendered to God. God must be our end. To please Him must be our aim in everything, or we sin.

– 10 –
How to Overcome Sin

How to Overcome Sin

In every period of my ministerial life, I have found many professed Christians in a miserable state of bondage, either to the world, the flesh, or the Devil. But surely this is not a Christian state, for the apostle distinctly said, *"Sin shall not have dominion over you: for ye are not under the law, but under grace"* (Romans 6:14).

A False Approach to Overcoming Sin

In all my Christian life, I have been pained to find so many Christians living in the legal bondage described in the seventh chapter of Romans—a life of sinning, resolving to reform, and falling again. And what is particularly saddening, and even agonizing, is that many ministers and leading Christians give completely false instruction on how to overcome sin. The directions that are generally given on this subject, I am sorry to say, amount to this: "Take your sins in detail, resolve to abstain from them, and fight against them, if need be with prayer and fasting, until you have overcome them.

Set your will firmly against a relapse into sin, pray and struggle, and resolve that you will not fall—and persist in this until you form the habit of obedience and break all your sinful habits." To be sure, it is generally added, "In this conflict, you must not depend upon your own strength but pray for the help of God." In a word, much of the teaching, both of the pulpit and the Christian press really amounts to this: sanctification is by works, and not by faith.

I notice that Dr. Chalmers, in his lectures on Romans, expressly maintains that justification is by faith but sanctification is by works. Some twenty-five years ago, I think, a prominent professor of theology in New England maintained in essence the same doctrine. In my early Christian life, I was very nearly misled by one of President Jonathan Edwards's resolutions. It was, in substance, that when he had fallen into any sin, he would trace it back to its source, and then fight and pray against it with all his might until he subdued it. This, it will be perceived, is directing the attention to the overt act of sin, its source or occasions. Resolving and fighting against it fastens the attention on the sin and its source, and diverts it entirely from Christ.

Now it is important to say right here that all such efforts are worse than useless and often result in delusion. First, when we do this, we lose sight of what really constitutes sin; second, we overlook the only practicable way to avoid it. In this way, the outward act or habit may be overcome and avoided, but what really constitutes the sin is left untouched.

Sin is not external but internal. It is not a muscular act; it is not the decision that causes a muscular action; it is not an involuntary feeling or desire. It is a voluntary act or state of mind. Sin is nothing else than that voluntary, ultimate preference or state of committal to self-pleasing out of which the decisions, the outward actions, purposes, intentions, and all the things that are commonly called sin proceed.

Now, what is resolved against in this religion of resolutions and efforts to suppress sinful habits and form holy habits? *"Love is the fulfilling of the law"* (Romans 13:10). But do we produce love by resolution? Do we eradicate selfishness by resolution? No, indeed. We may suppress this or that expression or manifestation of selfishness by resolving not to do this or that and by praying and struggling against it. We may resolve

> To try to obey God's commandments by personal resolution is an absurdity.

upon an outward obedience and work ourselves up to the letter of an obedience to God's commandments. But to eradicate selfishness from the heart by resolution is an absurdity. So, the effort to obey the commandments of God in spirit—in other words, to attempt to love as the law of God requires—by force of resolution is an absurdity.

There are many who maintain that sin consists in the desires. Be it so. Do we control our desires by force of resolution? We may abstain from the *gratification* of a particular desire by the force of resolution. We may go further and abstain from the gratification of desire generally in the outward life. But this is not to obtain the love of God, which constitutes obedience. If we should become secluded monks, lock ourselves in a cell, and crucify all our desires and appetites so far as their indulgence is concerned, we have only avoided certain forms of sin; but the root that really constitutes sin is not touched. Our resolution has not secured love, which is the only real obedience to God. All our battling with sin in the outward life by the force of resolution only ends in making us whitened sepulchers. All our battling with desire by the force of resolution is of no avail. In all this, however successful the effort to suppress sin may be in the outward life or in the inward desire, it will end only in delusion, for by force of resolution we cannot love.

Sin Is Overcome Only by Faith in Christ

All such efforts to overcome sin are utterly futile and as unscriptural as they are futile. The Bible expressly teaches us that sin is overcome by faith in Christ: "[He] *is made unto us wisdom, and righteousness, and sanctification, and redemption*" (1 Corinthians 1:30). "[He is] *the way, the truth, and the life*" (John 14:6). Christians are said to "[purify] *their hearts by faith*" (Acts 15:9). And in Acts 26:18, it is affirmed that the saints are *"sanctified by faith"* in Christ. In Romans 9:31–32, it is affirmed that the Jews did not attain to righteousness *"because they sought it not by faith, but as it were by the works of the law."*

The doctrine of the Bible is that Christ saves His people from sin through faith, that Christ's Spirit is received by faith to dwell in the heart. It is faith that works by love (Galatians 5:6). Love is wrought and sustained by faith. By faith, Christians overcome the world, the flesh, and the Devil. It is by faith that they *"quench all the fiery darts of the evil one"* (Ephesians 6:16 RV). It is by faith that they *"put on Christ"* (Galatians 3:27) and *"put off the old man with his deeds"* (Colossians 3:9). It is by faith that we *"fight the good fight"* (1 Timothy 6:12), and not by resolution. It is *"by faith* [we] *stand"* (2 Corinthians 1:24); by resolution we fall. *"This is the victory that overcometh the world, even our faith"* (1 John 5:4). It is by faith that the flesh is kept under control and carnal desires subdued. The fact is that it is simply by faith that we receive the Spirit of Christ to work in us *"to will and to do* [according to] *his good pleasure"* (Philippians 2:13). He sheds abroad His own love in our hearts and thereby kindles ours. (See Romans 5:5.)

Every victory over sin is by faith in Christ. Whenever the mind is diverted from Christ by resolving and fighting against sin, whether we are aware of it or not, we are acting in our own strength; we are rejecting the help of Christ and are under a specious delusion. Nothing but the life and energy of the Spirit of Christ within us can save us from sin, and trust is the uniform and universal condition of the working of this saving energy within us.

> One of the hardest lessons for us is to renounce self-dependence and trust wholly in Christ.

How long will this fact be at least practically overlooked by the teachers of religion? How deeply rooted in the heart of man is self-righteousness and self-dependence? It is rooted so deeply that one of the hardest lessons for the human heart to learn is to renounce self-dependence and trust wholly in Christ. When we open the door by implicit trust, He enters in and takes up His abode with us and in us. By shedding abroad His love, He quickens our whole souls into harmony with Himself, and in this way—and in this way alone—He purifies our hearts through faith. He sustains our will in the attitude of devotion. He quickens and regulates our affections, desires, appetites, and passions, and becomes our sanctification. Much of the teaching that we hear in prayer and conference meetings, from the pulpit and the press, is so misleading as to render the hearing or reading of such instruction almost too painful to be endured. Such instruction is guaranteed to produce delusion, discouragement, and a practical rejection of Christ as He is presented in the Gospel.

Alas for the blindness that bewilders the soul that is longing after deliverance from the power of sin! I have sometimes listened to legal teaching on this subject until I felt as if I would scream. It is astonishing sometimes to hear Christian men object to the teaching that I have here set forth—that it leaves us in a passive state to be saved without our own activity. What darkness is involved in this objection! The Bible teaches that by trusting in Christ, we receive an inward influence that stimulates and directs our activity. It teaches that by faith we receive His purifying influence into the very center of our being. Through and by His truth revealed directly to the soul, He quickens our whole inward being into the attitude of loving obedience. This is the way, the only practicable way, to overcome sin.

True Sanctification

But someone may say, "Does not the apostle exhort us to 'work out our salvation with fear and trembling, because it is God who works in us, both to will and to do of His good pleasure'? And is not this an exhortation to do what you here condemn?" By no means. Paul said in Philippians 2:12–13:

> *Wherefore, my beloved, as ye have always obeyed, not as in my presence only, but now much more in my absence, work out your own salvation with fear and trembling. For it is God which worketh in you both to will and to do of his good pleasure.*

This passage does not exhort us to work by force of resolution, but through and by the in-working of God. Paul had taught them, while he was present with them; but now, in his absence, he exhorts them to work out their own salvation, not by resolution but by the inward operation of God. This is precisely the doctrine of this chapter. Paul often taught the church that Christ in the heart is our sanctification and that this influence is to be received by faith. He taught this too often to be guilty in this passage of teaching that our sanctification is to be worked out by resolution and efforts to suppress sinful habits and form holy ones.

This passage of Scripture happily recognizes both the divine and human agency in the work of sanctification. God works in us to will and to do; and we, accepting by faith His in-working, will and do according to His good pleasure. Faith itself is an active and not a passive state. A passive holiness is impossible and absurd. Let no one say that when we exhort people to trust wholly in Christ, we teach that anyone should be or can be passive in receiving and cooperating with the divine influence within. This influence is moral and not physical. It is persuasion and not force. It influences the free will and, consequently, does this by truth and not by force.

Oh, that it could be understood that the whole of the spiritual life that is in *any* man is received directly from the Spirit of Christ by faith, as the branch receives its life from the vine! (See John 15:4–5.) Away with this religion of resolutions! It is a snare of death. Away with this effort to make the life holy while the heart does not have in it the love of God! Oh, that we would learn to look directly at Christ through the Gospel, and so embrace Him by an act of loving trust that our whole beings would be in harmony with His state of mind. This, and this alone, is sanctification.

THE DECAY OF CONSCIENCE

– 11 –

The Decay of Conscience

I believe it is a fact generally admitted that there is much less conscience manifested by men and women of nearly all walks of life than there was forty years ago. There is justly much complaint of this, and there seems to be but little prospect of reformation. The rings and frauds and villainies in high and low places, among all ranks of men, are so alarming that one is almost compelled to ask, "Can nobody be safely trusted?" Now, what is the cause of this degeneracy? No doubt, there are many causes that contribute more or less directly to it, but I am persuaded that the fault is more in the ministry and the public press than in any and all things else.

It has been fashionable now for many years to ridicule and decry Puritanism. Ministers have ceased, in a great measure, to probe the consciences of men with the spiritual law of God. So far as my knowledge extends, there has been a great letting down and an ignoring of the searching claims of God's law as revealed in His Word. This law is the only standard of true morality. *"By the law is the knowledge of sin"* (Romans 3:20). The law is the quickener of the human conscience. As much as the spirituality of the law of God is kept out of view, that is how much there will be a decay of conscience. This must be the inevitable result. Let ministers ridicule Puritanism and attempt to preach the Gospel without thoroughly probing the conscience with the divine law, and this must result in, at least, a partial paralysis of the moral sense.

The error that lies at the foundation of this decay of individual and public conscience originates, no doubt, in the pulpit. The proper guardians of the public conscience have, I fear, very much neglected to expound and insist on obedience to the moral law. It is plain that some of our most popular preachers are phrenologists.[*] Phrenology has no organ of free will. Hence, it has no moral agency, no moral law, and no moral obligation in any proper sense of these terms. A consistent phrenologist can have no proper ideas of moral obligation, moral guilt, blameworthiness, or retribution.

Some years ago, a brother of one of our most popular preachers heard me preach on the text, *"Be ye reconciled to God"* (2 Corinthians 5:20). I showed, among other things, that being reconciled to God implies being reconciled to the execution of His law. He visited me the next morning and among other things said that neither he nor two of his brothers whom he named, all preachers, naturally had any conscience. "We have," said he, "no such ideas in our minds of sin, guilt, justice, and

---

[*] Phrenology was a system in which character was supposedly determined by studying the shape of the skull.

retribution as our father and you have. We cannot preach as you do on those subjects." He continued, "I am striving to cultivate a conscience, and I think I begin to understand what it is. But naturally, neither I nor the two brothers I have named have any conscience."

Now, these three ministers have repeatedly set their writings before the public. I have read much that they have written, and not infrequently the sermons of one of them. I have been struck with the obvious lack of conscience in his sermons and writings. He is a phrenologist; hence, he has in his theological views no free will, no moral agency, and nothing that is really a logical result of free will and moral agency. He can ridicule Puritanism and the great doctrines of the orthodox faith; indeed, his whole teaching, so far as it has fallen under my eye, most lamentably shows the lack of moral discrimination. I should judge from his writings that the true ideas of moral depravity, guilt, and deserved punishment, in the true acceptation of those terms, have no place in his mind. Indeed, as a consistent phrenologist, such ideas have no right in his mind. They are necessarily excluded by his philosophy.

I do not know how extensively phrenology has poisoned the minds of ministers of different denominations, but I have observed with pain that many ministers who write for the public press fail to reach the consciences of men. They fail to go to the bottom of the matter and fail to insist on obedience to the moral law as alone acceptable to God. They seem to me to *make void the law through faith* (Romans 3:31). They seem to hold up a different standard from what is taught in Christ's Sermon on the Mount, which was Christ's exposition of the moral law. Christ expressly taught that there is no salvation without conformity to the rule of life laid down in that sermon. True faith in Christ will always and inevitably produce a holy life. But I fear it has become fashionable to preach what amounts to an antinomian gospel.* The rule of life proclaimed in the Gospels is precisely that of the moral law. These four things are expressly affirmed of true faith—of the faith of the New Testament:

> True faith in Christ will always and inevitably produce a holy life.

- ◆ It establishes the law (Romans 3:31).
- ◆ It works by love (Galatians 5:6).
- ◆ It purifies the heart (Acts 15:9).
- ◆ It overcomes the world (1 John 5:4).

These are but different forms of affirming that true faith does, as a matter of fact, produce a holy life. If it did not, it would make the law void. The true Gospel is not preached where obedience to the moral law as the only rule of life is not insisted on. Wherever there is a failure to do this in the instructions of any pulpit, it will inevitably be seen that the hearers of such a mutilated message will have very little conscience. We need more Boanerges, that is,

---

* This is the belief that the moral law is not needed because only faith is necessary for salvation.

"sons of thunder" (Mark 3:17), in the pulpit. We need men who will flash forth the law of God like livid lightning and arouse the consciences of men. We need more Puritanism in the pulpit. To be sure, some of the Puritans were extremists. But still, under their teaching there was a very different state of the individual and public conscience from what exists in these days. Those old, stern, grand vindicators of the government of God would have rained down thunder and lightning until they had almost demolished their pulpits if any such immoralities had shown themselves under their instructions as are common in these days.

In a great measure, the periodical press takes its tone from the pulpit. The universal literature of the present day shows conclusively that the moral sense of the people needs toning up, and some of our most fascinating preachers have become the favorites of infidels, skeptics of every grade, universalists, and the most wicked characters. And has *"the offence of the cross ceased"* (Galatians 5:11), or is the cross kept out of view? Has the holy law of God, with its stringent precepts and its dreadful penalty, become popular with unsaved men and women? Or is it ignored in the pulpit and the preacher praised for that neglect of duty for which he should be despised? I believe the only possible way to arrest this downward tendency in private and public morals is the holding up from the pulpits in this land, with unsparing faithfulness, the whole Gospel of God, including as the only rule of life the perfect and holy law of God.

The holding up of this law will reveal the moral depravity of the heart, and the holding forth of the cleansing blood of Christ will cleanse the heart from sin. Is there not a great lack of preaching on this subject? Preachers are *"set for the defence of the* [blessed] *gospel"* (Philippians 1:17) and for the vindication of God's holy law. I implore them to probe the consciences of our hearers, to thunder forth the law and Gospel of God until their voices reach the Capitol of this nation through our representatives in Congress.

It is now very common for even the secular papers to publish extracts of sermons. Preachers should give the reporters of the press such work to do as will make their ears and the ears of their readers tingle. Let our railroad magnates, our stock gamblers, our officials of every rank, hear from its widespread pulpit, if they come within the sound, such wholesome Puritanic preaching that will arouse them to better thoughts and a better life. Away with this milk-and-water preaching of a love of Christ that has no holiness or moral discrimination in it. Away with preaching a love of God that is not angry with sinners every day. Away with preaching a Christ not crucified for sin.

Christ crucified for the sins of the world is the Christ that the people need. Preachers should rid themselves of the just accusation of neglecting to preach the law of God until the consciences of men are asleep. Such a collapse of conscience in this land could never have existed if the Puritan element in their preaching had not to a great extent been left out.

Some years ago, I was preaching to a congregation whose pastor had died some months before. He seemed to have been almost universally popular with his church and the community. His church seemed to have nearly idolized him. Everybody was speaking praise of him and holding him up as an example; and yet both the church and the community clearly demonstrated that they had had an unfaithful minister, a man who loved and sought the applause of his people. I heard so much of his teachings and saw so much of the legitimate fruits of his teachings that I felt constrained to tell the people from the pulpit that they had had an unfaithful minister. I told them that such fruits as were apparent on every side, both within and outside that church, could never have resulted from a faithful presentation of the Gospel. This assertion would, no doubt, have greatly shocked them had it been made under other circumstances; but, since the way had been prepared, they did not seem disposed to deny it.

> The Fruits Test:
> Faithless preaching produces bad fruits, but faithful preaching produces good fruits.

Preaching will bear its legitimate fruits. If immorality prevails in the land, it is the preachers' fault to a great degree. If there is a decay of conscience, the pulpit is responsible for it. If the public press lacks moral discrimination, the pulpit is responsible for it. If the church is degenerate and worldly, the pulpit is responsible for it. If the world loses its interest in religion, the pulpit is responsible for it. If Satan rules in our halls of legislation, the pulpit is responsible for it. If our politics become so corrupt that the very foundations of our government are ready to fall away, the pulpit is responsible for it. Preachers should not ignore this fact, but should take it to heart, and be thoroughly awake to their responsibility concerning the morals of this nation.

– 12 –
THE PSYCHOLOGY OF FAITH

– 12 –

The Psychology of Faith

I have heretofore tried to show that sanctification is worked in the soul by the Spirit of Christ, through faith, not without but with our coopera-tion. I now wish to call attention to the nature or "psychology" of faith as a mental act or state. My theological teacher held that faith was an intellec-tual act or state, a conviction or firm persuasion that the doctrines of the Bible are true. As far as I can recall, this was the view of faith that I every-where heard advanced.

I heard an objection to this view. The objection was this: Intellectual convictions and states are involuntary and so cannot be produced by any ef-fort of the will. Consequently, if faith were an in-tellectual act, it would also be involuntary, and we could not be expected to exercise faith. If this were the case, faith could not be a virtue. The reply to this objection was this: We control the attention of the mind by an effort of the will. Our responsibility, therefore, is to search for evidence that will con-vince the intellect. It was also replied that unbelief is a sin because it is the result of failing to search for and accept the evidence of the truth, and that faith is a virtue because it involves the consent and effort of the will to search out the truth.

A False Notion of Faith

I have met with this erroneous notion of the nature of Christian faith often since I was first licensed to preach. Especially in my early ministry, I found that great stress was laid on believing "the articles of faith," and it was held that faith consisted in believing with an unwavering conviction the doctrines about Christ. Hence, an acceptance of the doctrines, the *doctrines,* the **doctrines** of the Gospel was very much insisted on as constituting faith. But I had been brought to accept these doctrines intellectually and firmly before I was converted. Therefore, when I was told to believe, I replied that I did believe—and no argument or assertion could convince me that I did not believe the Gospel. And up to the very moment of my conversion, I was not and could not be convinced of my error.

> Faith is more than an intellectual affirmation of doctrines about Christ; it is trust in His person.

At the moment of my conversion, or when I first exercised faith, I saw my ruinous error. I found that faith consisted not in an intellectual conviction that the things affirmed in the Bible about Christ are true, but in *the heart's trust in the person of Christ.* I learned that God's testimony concerning Christ was designed to lead me to trust Christ, to confide in His person as my Savior, and that to stop short in merely believing about Christ was a fatal mistake that inevitably left me in my sins.

It was as if I were sick almost unto death and someone recommended to me a physician who was surely able and willing to save my life. It was as if I had listened to the testimony concerning him until I was fully convinced that he was both able and willing to save my life, and then was told to believe in him and my life would be secure. Now, if I understood this to mean nothing more than to accept the testimony with the firmest conviction, I would reply, "I do believe in him with an undoubting faith. I believe every word you have told me regarding him." But if I stopped here, I would, of course, lose my life. In addition to this firm intellectual conviction of his willingness and ability, it would be essential to request his help, to come to him, to trust his person, to accept his treatment. When I had intellectually accepted the testimony concerning him with an unwavering belief, the next and the indispensable thing would be a voluntary act of trust or confidence in his person, a committal of my life to him and his sovereign treatment in the cure of my disease.

The True Nature of Faith

Now, this illustrates the true nature or psychology of faith as it actually exists in consciousness. It does not consist in any degree of intellectual knowledge or acceptance of the doctrines of the Bible. The firmest possible persuasion that every word said in the Bible respecting God and Christ is true is not faith. These truths and doctrines reveal God in Christ only so far as they point to God in Christ and teach the soul how to find Him by an act of trust in His person.

When we firmly trust in His person and commit our souls to Him by an unwavering act of confidence in Him for all that He is affirmed to be to us in the Bible, this is faith. We trust Him upon the testimony of God. We trust Him for what the doctrines and facts of the Bible declare Him to be to us. This act of trust unites our spirit to Him in a union so close that we directly receive from Him a current of eternal life. Faith, in consciousness, seems to complete the divine galvanic circle, and the life of God is instantly imparted to our souls. God's life and light and love and peace and joy seem to flow to us as naturally and spontaneously as the galvanic current from the battery. For the first time, we then understand what Christ meant by our being united to Him by faith as the branch is united to the vine. Christ is then and thus revealed to us as God. We are conscious of direct communion with Him, and we know Him as we know ourselves by His direct activity within us. We then know directly, in consciousness, that He is our life, and that we receive from Him, moment by moment, as it were, an impartation of eternal life.

With some, the mind is comparatively dark, and their faith, therefore, is comparatively weak in its first exercise. They may hold a great breadth of opinion and yet intellectually believe but little with clear conviction. Hence, their trust in Him will be as narrow as their convictions. When faith is weak, the current of the divine life will flow so mildly that we are scarcely conscious of it. But when faith is strong and all-embracing, it lets a current of the divine life of love into our souls so strong that it seems to permeate both soul and body. We then know in consciousness what it is to have Christ's Spirit within us as a power to save us from sin and keep our feet in the path of loving obedience.

Stopping Short of Faith in Christ

From personal conversation with hundreds— and I may say thousands—of Christian people, I have been struck with the application of Christ's words, as recorded in the fifth chapter of John, to their experience. Christ said to the Jews,

> [You] *search the scriptures* [for so it should be rendered]; *for in them ye think ye have eternal life: and they are they which testify of me. And ye will not come to me, that ye might have life.*   (John 5:39–40)

They stopped short in the Scriptures. They satisfied themselves with ascertaining what the Scriptures said *about* Christ but did not use the light thus received to come to Him by an act of loving trust in His person. I fear it is true in these days, as it has been in the days that are past, that multitudes stop short in the facts and doctrines of the Bible. They do not, by any act of trust in Christ's person, come to Him, concerning whom all this testimony is given. Thus, the Bible is misunderstood and abused.

Many, understanding the Confession of Faith as summarizing the doctrines of the Bible, very much neglect the Bible and rest in a belief of the articles

> Multitudes stop short in merely the facts of the Bible.

143

of faith. Others, more cautious and more in earnest, search the Scriptures to see what they say about Christ, but stop short and rest in the formation of correct theological opinions. But others, and they are the only saved class, love the Scriptures intensely because they testify of Jesus. They search and devour the Scriptures because they tell them who Jesus is and what they may trust Him for. They do not stop short and rest in this testimony, but by an act of loving trust go directly to Him—to His person—thus joining their souls to Him. This joining forms a union that receives from Him, by a direct divine communication, the things for which they are led to trust Him. This is certainly Christian experience. This is receiving from Christ the eternal life that God has given to us in Him. This is saving faith.

There are many degrees in the strength of faith: from that of which we are hardly conscious to that which lets such a flood of eternal life into the soul as to quite overcome the strength of the body. In the strongest exercise of faith, the nerves of the body seem to give way for the time being under the over- whelming exercise of the mind. This great strength of mental exercise is perhaps not very common. We can endure but little of God's light and love in our souls and yet remain in our bodies. I have some- times felt that a little clearer vision would draw my soul entirely away from the body, and I have met with many Christian people to whom these strong gales of spiritual influence were familiar. However, my object in writing this is to illustrate the nature or psychology and results of saving faith.

The contemplation of the attitude and experi- ence of numbers of professed Christians in regard to Christ brings surprise and disappointment, considering that the Bible is in their hands. Many of them appear to have stopped short in theological *opinions* more or less firmly held. This they understand to be faith. Others are more in earnest, and they stop not short of a more or less certain *conviction* of the truths of the Bible concerning Christ. Others have strong impressions of the *obligations* of the law, which move them to begin an earnest life of works—which leads them into bondage. They pray from a sense of duty; they are dutiful, but not loving, not confiding. They have no peace and no rest, except in cases where they persuade themselves that they have done their duty. They are in a restless, agonizing state.

> Reason they hear, her counsels weigh,
>   And all her words approve,
> And yet they find it hard to obey,
>   And harder still to love.

They read and perhaps search the Scriptures to learn their duty and to learn about Christ. They intellectually believe all that they understand the Scriptures to say about Him. But when Christ is thus commended to their confidence, they do not by an act of personal commitment to Him so join their souls to Him as to receive the influx of His life and light and love. They do not, by a simple act of personal loving trust in His person, receive the current of His divine life and power into their own souls. They do not thus take hold of His strength and interlock their being with His. In other words, they do not truly believe. Hence, they are not saved.

Oh, what a mistake this is! I fear it is very common. No, it seems to be certain that it is appallingly common, or else how can the state of the church be accounted for? Is what we see in the great mass of church members *all* that Christ does for and in His people when they truly believe? No, no! There is great error here. The psychology of faith is mistaken, and an intellectual conviction of the truth of the Gospel is supposed to be faith. And some whose opinions seem to be right in regard to the nature of faith rest in their philosophy and fall short of *exercising* faith.

Let no one suppose that I underestimate the value of the facts and doctrines of the Bible. I regard a knowledge and belief of them as of fundamental importance. I have no sympathy with those who undervalue them and treat doctrinal discussion and preaching as of minor importance, nor can I assent to the teaching of those who would have us preach Christ and not the doctrines respecting Him. It is the facts and doctrines of the Bible that teach us who Christ is, why He is to be trusted, and for what He is to be trusted. How can we preach Christ without preaching *about* Him? And how can we trust Him without being informed why and for what we are to trust Him?

> The error is in stopping short of trusting the personal Christ.

The error to which I call attention does not consist in laying too much stress on teaching and believing the facts and doctrines of the Word. No, it consists in stopping short of trusting the personal Christ for what those facts and doctrines teach us to trust Him. It consists in satisfying ourselves with believing the testimony concerning Him, thus resting in the belief of what God has said about Him instead of committing our souls to Him by an act of loving trust.

Trusting Christ Implicitly

The testimony of God respecting Him is designed to secure our confidence in Him. If it fails to secure the uniting of our souls to Him by an act of implicit trust in Him—such an act of trust as unites us to Him as the branch is united to the vine—we have heard the Gospel in vain. We are not saved. We have failed to receive from Him that impartation of eternal life, which can be conveyed to us through no other channel than that of implicit trust.

– 13 –
THE PSYCHOLOGY OF RIGHTEOUSNESS

THE PSYCHOLOGY OF
RIGHTEOUSNESS

During my Christian life, I have been asked a great many times, in substance, by thoughtful and anxious souls, "What is the mental act and state (or the acts and states) that God requires of me?" I have found it profitable, even indispensable, with the commands of God before me, to find a satisfactory answer to this question. I have satisfied myself, and, by the help of God, I trust I have aided many others to their satisfaction. Be it understood, then, that by "the psychology of righteousness" I mean the mental act and state that constitutes righteousness. I will try to develop this theme by showing:

♦ What righteousness is not
♦ What righteousness is
♦ How we know what righteousness is
♦ How a sinner may attain to righteousness

What Righteousness Is Not

Righteousness does not consist of anything in the outward life or in any physical or bodily act whatever. All such acts belong to the category of cause and effect. They are caused by an act of the will and have in themselves no moral character whatever.

Righteousness does not consist in volition. Volition—deciding and resolving to do something—is an act of will, but it is caused by choice. It is the product of a purpose or choice; it is an act of carrying out. It is designed as a means to an end. It is put forth to control either the intellect, the emotions, or the actions by force.

Volition is both an effect and a cause. It is the effect of a choice, purpose, intention. It is the cause of the outward life and of many of the changes both of the intellect and emotions.

Volition is a doing. Whatever we do, we accomplish by the exercise of volition.

Volition is not, in the highest sense, a free act, because it is an effect. It is itself caused. Hence, it has no moral character in itself, and moral quality can be attributed to it only by looking at its primary cause.

Righteousness does not consist in proximate or subordinate choice, which is a choice that is made in order to bring about a particular end.

Ultimate choice, on the other hand, is choosing an ultimate, supreme end *for its own sake.* Such choice does not bring about a particular end. It is not put forth to secure the end but is simply the choice of an object for its own sake.

Subordinate or proximate choice, as already stated, is purposing or choosing to secure a particular end, if possible. Strictly speaking, this choice belongs (like volition) to the category of cause and effect. It results by necessity from the ultimate choice. In the strictest sense, it is not a free act, since it is itself caused. Hence, it has no moral character in itself but, like volition, derives whatever moral quality it has from its primary cause or the ultimate choice.

Righteousness does not consist in any of the states or activities of the sensibility. (By the sensibility I mean that department of the mind that feels, desires, suffers, enjoys.) All the states of the sensibility are involuntary and belong to the category of cause and effect. The will cannot control them directly, nor can it always control them indirectly. This we know by consciousness. Since they are caused and not free, they can have no moral character in themselves. Like thoughts, volitions, and subordinate choices, they have no moral quality except that which is derived from their primary cause.

> Righteousness is moral rightness.

In short, righteousness does not consist in doing anything, resolving anything, choosing anything for any secondary purpose, or in any feeling of desire, remorse, or ecstasy. None of these means can secure or produce righteousness.

What Righteousness Is

Righteousness is moral rightness, moral rectitude, moral uprightness, conformity to moral law. How do we conform to moral law? What mental act or state is required by the moral law, the law of God? Law is a rule of action. Moral law requires action—mental action, responsible action, therefore free action. But what particular *form* of action does moral law require?

Free action is a certain form of action of the will (and this is the only strictly free action). Christ has taught us, by His own teaching and through His inspired prophets and apostles, that the moral law requires love, and that this is the sum of its requirements. But what is this love? It cannot be the involuntary love of the sensibility, either in the form of emotion or affection; for these states of mind, belonging as they do to the category of cause and effect, cannot be the form of love demanded by the law of God.

The moral law is the law of God's activity, the rule in conformity to which He always acts. We are created in God's image; His rule of life is therefore ours. The moral law requires of Him the *same* kind of love that it does of us. (If God had no law or rule of action, He could have no moral character.) As our Creator and Lawgiver, He requires of us the same kind of love and the same degree of perfection that He Himself exercises. *"God is love"* (1 John 4:8). This means He loves with all the strength of His infinite nature. He requires us to love with all the strength of our finite nature. This is being perfect as God is perfect (Matthew 5:48).

But what is this love of God (that is, as a mental exercise)? It must be benevolence or good will, for God is a moral agent. The good of universal being is infinitely valuable in itself. God must infinitely well appreciate this. He must see and feel the moral propriety of choosing this for its own sake. He has chosen it from eternity. By His executive volitions He is endeavoring to realize it. The law that He has established to govern our activity requires us to be in harmony with His choice, His benevolence. It requires us to choose the same end that He does, for the same reason—that is, *for its own sake.*

God's infinite choice of the good of universal being is righteousness in Him, because it is the choice of the intrinsically and infinitely valuable for its own sake. It is a choice in conformity with His nature and the relations He has constituted. It must be a choice in conformity with His infinitely clear conscience or moral sense. Righteousness in God, then, is conformity to the laws of universal love or good will. It must be an ultimate, supreme, inherent, effective preference or choice of the highest good of universal being, including His own. It must be ultimate in that this good of being is chosen for its own sake. It must be supreme because it is preferred to everything else. It must be inherent because it is innate and at the very foundation of all His moral activity. It must be effective because, from its very nature, it must energize to secure that which is thus preferred or chosen with the whole strength of His infinite nature. This is right choice, right moral action.

The moral quality, then, of *unselfish benevolence* is righteousness or moral rightness. All subordinate choices, volitions, actions, and states of sensibility that proceed from unselfish benevolence have moral character. They have moral character in the sense and only for the reason that they proceed from or are the natural product of unselfish benevolence. This ultimate, inherent, supreme preference is the holy heart of a moral agent. Out of it proceeds, directly or indirectly, the whole moral or spiritual life of the individual.

How We Know What Righteousness Is

We know what righteousness is by consciousness. By consciousness, we know that our whole life proceeds from ultimate choice or preference. By consciousness, we know that the conscience demands perfect, universal love or unselfish benevolence. And, therefore, conscience demands all those acts and states of mind and outward actions of life that by a law of our nature proceed from unselfish benevolence. By consciousness, we know that the conscience is satisfied with this, demands nothing more, and accepts nothing less. By consciousness, we know that the conscience pronounces this to be right or righteousness. By consciousness, we know that this is obedience to the law of God as revealed in our nature, and that when we render this obedience, we are so adjusted in the will of God that we have perfect peace. We are in harmony with God. We are at peace with God and with ourselves. Short of this, we cannot be so.

> Obedience to God's law brings perfect peace.

This I understand to be the teaching both of our nature and the Bible. My limits will not allow me to quote Scripture to sustain this view.

How a Sinner May Attain to Righteousness

A sinner is a selfish moral agent. Being selfish, he will, of course, make no other than selfish efforts to become righteous. Selfishness is a state of voluntary commitment to the indulgence of the sensibility. While the will is in this state of commitment to self-indulgence, the soul will not and cannot put forth any righteous act. The first righteous act possible to an unregenerate sinner is to change his heart, or the supreme, ultimate preference of his soul. Without this he may outwardly conform to the letter of God's law, but this is not righteousness. Without this he may have many exercises and states of mind that he may suppose to be Christian experiences, but these are not righteousness. He may even live a perfectly outwardly moral and religious life without a change of heart. All this he may do for selfish reasons, but *this is not righteousness.*

I say again, his first righteous act must be to change his heart. To say that he will change this for any selfish reason is simply a contradiction, for the change of heart involves the renunciation of selfishness. How, then, can a sinner change his heart or attain to righteousness? My answer is, Only by taking such a view of the character and claims of God as to induce him to renounce his self-seeking spirit and come into harmony with God.

To say nothing here of possibility, the Bible reveals the fact (and human consciousness attests the truth) that a sinner will never attain this view on his own. He will never attain to a view of the claims of God that will induce him to renounce selfishness and come to God without the illuminations of the Holy Spirit. A sinner attains, then, to righteousness *only* through the teachings and inspirations of the Holy Spirit.

But what is involved in this change from sin to righteousness? It must involve confidence in God, or faith. Without confidence, a soul could not be persuaded to change his heart, renounce self, and come to God. It must involve repentance. By repentance I mean that change of mind that consists in a renunciation of self-seeking and a coming into harmony with God. It involves a radical change of moral attitude in respect to God and our neighbors. All three of these are involved in a change of heart. They occur simultaneously, and the presence of one implies the existence and presence of the others.

It is by the truths of the Gospel that the Holy Spirit induces this change in sinful man. This revelation of divine love, when powerfully sent home by the Holy Spirit, is an effective calling. From the above it will be seen that, although a sinner may live a perfectly outwardly moral and religious life, a truly regenerated soul cannot live a sinful life. The new heart does not, cannot, sin. John in his first epistle clearly affirms this. A benevolent, supreme, ultimate choice cannot produce selfish subordinate choices or volitions.

> Righteousness is sustained only by the indwelling of Christ through faith.

It is possible for a Christian to backslide. If it were not, perseverance would be no virtue. If the change were a physical one or a change of the very nature of the sinner, backsliding would be impossible and perseverance no virtue. There is an objection to this view that backsliding must consist in going back to a selfish ultimate preference, and, therefore, involve an adverse change of heart. What if it does? Must this not be, indeed, true? Did not Adam and Eve change their hearts from holy to sinful ones?

But may a man change his heart back and forth? My answer is, Yes, or a sinner could not be required to choose for himself a new heart, nor could a Christian sin after regeneration. The idea that the same person can have at the same time both a holy and a sinful heart is absurd in true philosophy, contrary to the Bible, and of a most pernicious tendency. When a soul is backslidden, Christ calls upon him to repent and do his first work over again.

Righteousness is sustained in the human soul by the indwelling of Christ through faith—and in no other way. It cannot be sustained by purposes or resolutions self-originated and not worked in us by the Spirit of Christ. Through faith Christ first gains ascendancy in the human heart, and through faith He maintains this ascendancy and reigns as King in the soul.

There can be no righteousness in man back of his heart, for nothing back of this can be voluntary; therefore, there can be no righteousness in the nature of man in the sense that implies praiseworthiness or virtue.

All outward conformity to the law and commandments of God that does not proceed from Christ, working in the soul by His Holy Spirit, is *self*-righteousness. All *true* righteousness, then, is the righteousness of faith, or a righteousness obtained by Christ through faith in Him.